Praise for

*Again*

"While never having had cancer, *Again* made me smile often and become teary a few times. The look at cancer through a young person's and a grown women's experience are enlightening, the practical suggestions gentle and personable, the love between the author and her husband inspiring. This is a full, honest book worth more than one read."

*Helen Addison*

Editor, *Paul Shulenburg: Oil Paintings*, and Owner of Addison Art Gallery

"Courageous writing that blends realism and optimism. This story is a faithful companion on a difficult journey."

*Lorraine Ash*

Author, *Life Touches Life: A Mother's Story of Stillbirth and Healing*

"Using deadpan humor and her fierce intellect, Chris Corrigan turns an unflinching eye on her second experience with cancer, weaving the past and present together to uncover and address long hidden patterns. This isn't your typical 'cancer book.' It's a book about the stories we're told about ourselves and how, true or false, they shape us, and how these stories, when faced and integrated, can be transformed into entirely new narratives. Survival is not about the diagnosis. Survival is about the life we create from what we're given."

*Laraine Herring*

Author, *A Constellation of Ghosts: A Speculative Memoir with Ravens*

"If you have been given a cancer diagnosis, this book will feel like a friend clasping your hand warmly with guidance and support."

*Jacqui Boulter*

Author, *Where Horses Fly*

"*Again* isn't only the story of Christine Corrigan's courageous two time encounter with cancer (aka *the Beast*). It is also a roadmap for the soft skills that are critical for cancer patients, survivors, medical teams and caregivers to develop in order to build and maintain the highest quality of life for those burdened by cancer through treatment and well into survivorhood. Christine has opened herself and intimately shared her story, and in doing so has gifted all of us with the life wisdom, knowledge, power and tips that she labored so hard to gain from life's adversity."

*Nora McMahon*

Founder, Cancergrad.org

"Weaving her vastly different cancer experiences as a teen and an adult, Chris Corrigan provides a compelling road map for newly diagnosed cancer patients and their caregivers. She deftly combines her grief over her losses with moments of humor, her desire for control and eventual acceptance of her village's help, and her anxiety over cancer's uncertainty and discovery of a path to peace, as well as practical guidance gained from experience."

*Dana Holwitt, MD, FACS*

Breast Surgeon and Breast Cancer Survivor

"*Again* takes on the tough subject of cancer with a direct, no-nonsense style, and offers the wisdom of one who has fought 'the beast' twice. With unflinching honesty about the realities of treatment in 1981 and now, Corrigan offers insight for cancer patients and their loved ones, as well as her humor, resilience, and courage. We also come to know the vibrant and loving community that carries her through, because, as she is told early on, 'None of us ever goes through this alone.' With *Again,* Corrigan offers an important voice, guiding patients as they take face this harrowing journey.

*Joanell Serra*

Author, *The Vines We Planted,* Co-editor, *(Her)oics: Women's Lived Experiences During the Coronavirus Pandemic*

"In *Again,* Christine Corrigan yanks us into the frightening heart of a midlife cancer diagnosis, holding the reader's hand with compassion, grit, a dollop of humor, and practical advice. Strengthened but also weakened by having once defeated the Beast as a teenager, when she had cancer but didn't know it, Corrigan's memoir is both calm elixir and potent provocation. Her story, of confronting medical secrets from her past, learning to accept help in the present, and battling for a future—all while trying to stay afloat as a mother, a professional in mid-career transition, wife, and person of faith—reaffirms all that we fear about the disease, but also all that we hope for about the human spirit. Perfect for the just-diagnosed woman, this book also speaks to anyone who wonders or cares about how we survive the worst life can throw at us, not once but twice."

*Lisa Romeo*

Author of *Starting with Goodbye: A Daughter's Memoir of Love After Loss*

"Christine Corrigan so seamlessly weaves her two cancer stories together bringing the reader on a journey through her life in a way that is both deeply personal yet practical. She provides information about the nuts and bolts of cancer treatments with a frankness that doesn't sugarcoat the often ugly details. Read this book if you are a cancer survivor or a friend to someone who has had cancer. You will laugh you will cry, and you will learn!"

*Paula Flory*

Executive Director, Move Over Breast Cancer Inc.

"Christine Corrigan writes in a clear, relatable, voice, at turns moving, hopeful, and funny. Alongside her story, Corrigan offers practical advice for navigating cancer diagnoses and treatment, sharing what she's learned along the way. More than an illness memoir, *Again* is a journey from adversity to acceptance and, ultimately happiness."

*Erin Khar*

Author of *STRUNG OUT: One Last Hit and Other Lies that Nearly Killed Me*

*Again:*
*Surviving Cancer Twice with Love and Lists*

*A Memoir*

By Christine Shields Corrigan

ISBN 978-1-64663-194-0

Library of Congress Control Number: 2020915350

Published by

**K köehlerbooks**™

3705 Shore Drive
Virginia Beach, VA 23455
800—435—4811
www.koehlerbooks.com

Kathy,

courage always ~

Christine Shields Corrigan

xo

# Christine Shields Corrigan

# Again

Surviving
Cancer Twice
with Love
and
Lists

VIRGINIA BEACH
CAPE CHARLES

For,


Tim, Kate, Tom, and James
My heart and my home, all roads lead to you.


In gratitude,

Muhammad R. Abbasi, M.D., Frank Forte, M.D. and
Athena Lee, P.A.
For lighting my path and leading me home.

"An individual doesn't get cancer, a family does."

—Terry Tempest Williams

# Table of Contents

*Part Three:* Closer to Fine

# Author's Note

OUR LIVES ARE MADE of stories, and our stories matter. This is a story about what happened to me, as best as I can remember it, and I have searched through journals, photographs, medical records, and conversations with those who were there to support it. I do not claim that this story is *the* truth. Our lives, including the very act of remembering, color our memories. Others who may have witnessed some of the events will have different recollections, or even no memory of them at all.

To protect privacy, some names and other information have been altered; some events have been compressed or merged for clarity. There are no composite characters.

On the journey to this book's creation, some of the material has appeared in short essays—under various titles and in different combinations or forms—in *Dreamers Creative Writing*; *Racked.com/Vox Media*; *The Potato Soup Journal*; and *Wildfire Magazine*.

The quote from *To Know by Experience* by Dan and Diane Meyer is reprinted with permission from The North Carolina Outward Bound School (Art Craft Press, 1973).

# Preface

WHEN FRIENDS AND FAMILY ask, *Why on earth did you write a book about having cancer, of all things?* I often reply, *Well, how much time do you have?*—Because the answer is complicated, and the answer is simple.

When I first heard the words that sent the car I was driving on my life's highway careening off the road and into a dark forest, I wanted a trail map. I wanted to know how I would face this disease again, not as a teen with parents, family, and friends who cared for me, but as a wife, mom, volunteer, and professional who had to care for others. I needed to make sure lunches were made, schedules kept, and deadlines met, all while dealing with chemotherapy, its side effects, surgeries, and their recoveries. I searched in bookstores, big and small, online, and in my local library for a book that would answer my burning question: how would I make it through?

I found plenty of books written by medical professionals about cancer, its diagnosis, and treatment. I didn't want medical information. I had, and continue to have, a fabulous team of medical professionals who know their stuff and whom I trust. I found celebrity cancer narratives. I'm not a celebrity and couldn't relate to their stories. I found beautiful memoirs about the meaning of life written by individuals who died—from cancer. While I've read many of them now, I could not contemplate reading them when I was newly diagnosed, terrified, and anxious. I found plenty of pink, *inspirational* guidebooks and journals. I didn't want to be inspired at the time. I wanted to rage and scream at the damn unfairness of a cancer diagnosis. I wanted the grit and truth of another's experience. I couldn't find that book.

I wanted to *fix* my experience like a compass needle to give a starting point and direction, as Louise DeSalvo suggests in *Writing to Heal,* so when the words no one ever wants to hear derails another's world, she will know she's not alone. That's why I wrote this book.

But that's not the only reason. I also wrote this book because I knew I would never recover unless I did. When I was a teen, I tried to give a voice to my cancer experiences, and my voice was silenced. I don't say that to ascribe blame, but in my family and school at that time, we didn't speak our feelings. We didn't acknowledge our fears. We dealt with what was and then moved on. My pathological ability to compartmentalize, organize, and avoid worked well for thirty-five years. Then it didn't. My systems crashed, burned, and shattered many of those whom I hold most precious, most dear.

This book gave me the grace to heal, to let go of old hurts and fears, and to forgive. This book also allowed me to grieve the life I once had and to move forward. Through this book, I mourned the loss of many taken too soon by this disease, including my cousins Nan Marie Astone and Peter Musacchio, and my father-in-law, Bob Corrigan. May their memories forever live and be a blessing.

This book made me pause and give thanks for the countless graces I received, not only while in treatment, but in the years that followed, and it opened my eyes to the vast inequity that exists in healthcare. I live near major medical centers and had access to the best medical care. Many don't. My family had the financial resources and insurance for my staggeringly expensive treatment and surgeries. Many don't. My outcome is indelibly tied to my socio-economic status and race. That's unconscionable and must change.

Finally, this book gave me the courage to step out of my planned and ordered life and to begin a practice that's led me to peaceful coexistence with life's awe and agony. None of us can escape loss, disease, aging, or our mortality. But perhaps, this book will help to light a path forward, as so many did for me.

# Part One

## STAND OR FALL

# Chapter 1
## On the Road Again

To Do (3/2)
Gym!
Groceries for Tom's birthday sleepover
Avoid kale
Order chocolate cake
Get cancer
Again

My hand hovered over the ringing wireless phone like it was the first time I'd ever answered it. I inhaled to push down the coldness creeping from my stomach to my chest. I answered the call as I walked from my desk into the darkened dining room adjacent to the kitchen so that I was out of earshot of my ten-year-old son, James, sitting at the counter doing his homework.

I slid down onto the oriental carpet and leaned back against one of the dining room chairs, my dark brown hair falling over my forehead. I pushed it back and bit my lip. I held the phone between my ear and shoulder and clenched my hands against my stomach while I prayed, *Please, please, please.*

"We have the biopsy results," my doctor said.

My doctor paused as my silent prayer raced heaven bound.

"And . . ." I stammered.

"I'm sorry to tell you, but you have a small, invasive ductal carcinoma in the right breast. We need to run some additional tests to come up with a treatment plan. The tests can take about a week or so."

"Oh, God." My heart, jolted by my body's adrenaline, pounded in my chest. I was ready to run, run anywhere, run from this news. I pulled myself to my feet from the dining room floor, walked back toward my desk and gripped its edge, hoping to draw strength from the cool soapstone under my fingers. The kitchen, with its cherry wood cabinets and cream-colored walls, glowed with the warmth that had left my body.

Three small words—*invasive ductal carcinoma*—and nothing, nothing would ever be the same. I knew this. I'd been running from *the Beast* since I was fourteen.

I willed myself not to cry, not with James in the kitchen, not with dinner on the stove. My porcini chicken simmered; the air was redolent of earthy mushrooms and shallots.

*Dear God. Come on! Wasn't once in a lifetime enough? Could we not do this again, please?*

"I know this is not the news you wanted, but we caught it early. I want you to schedule a breast MRI and ultrasound with Karen, my nurse."

I could see the doctor's kind, green eyes in my mind as he spoke. *This must be one of the most disheartening, yet courageous, things that doctors have to do*, I thought.

"I will. Thank you, Dr. Diehl."

I stood trembling at my desk as I replaced the phone in its stand. I didn't smoke. I didn't drink, at least not too much. I've tried to eat the right things, except kale because, well, it's kale. I worked out. *Why this? Why me? Why now?*

My eyes passed over the family photos crowding the shelves in the kitchen and family room. I blinked back my tears and summoned my strength to share this news with Tim, my husband of twenty-four years.

I walked down the hallway, painted soft gray, and grabbed the banister of the staircase opposite the glass French door leading into Tim's home office. For a moment, I watched Tim through the doors, his eyes intent on his computer screen, fingers flying across the keyboard.

Tim looked up from his screen in his familiar way and ran his hand over his temples, gray now. Sensing my presence, he glanced over at me, his eyes smiling behind his wire rim glasses, and waved. I opened the door and pressed it closed behind me.

My hazel eyes met his blue ones.

"What's wrong?"

The news tumbled from my mouth.

"That was Dr. Diehl. He had the biopsy results. It's invasive ductal carcinoma. Breast cancer. *Christ*," I gasped.

Tim's shoulders sagged. He stood. We walked over to each other, and he pulled me into his chest. His heart ricocheted on my cheek.

I knew Tim never forgave the doctors for not saving his dad, who had died from metastatic prostate cancer three years earlier. I was more forgiving of the doctors; it's the disease that's unforgiveable.

I looked into Tim's eyes, where tears were forming, and wiped them away, knowing full well I couldn't prevent the thundercloud of shit that was about to rain down on us.

"Hey, Dr. Diehl caught it early," I said. "He has to run more tests to figure the exact type it is and whether I will need chemo or surgery or both. It's going to take a week or so. We'll get through. A little faith, sweetie."

My words to Tim echoed my father's own words to me, said over three decades earlier when Dr. Forte shared my biopsy results with my parents and me in August 1981. At the time, I was fourteen.

⌐∽

"Kiddo, you have something called Hodgkin's disease, which is a type of blood disease and very treatable, but you are going to have a tough few months ahead."

I asked Dr. Forte the one and only question that popped into my teenage brain. "Am I going to die?"

"Yes," he replied, without missing a beat. "But not from this. You are going to need another operation, though, and a special a type of treatment called radiation therapy."

I threw myself into my parents' arms and could feel their sobs ripple through me. I knew the news was bad, because I never saw my parents cry.

I pulled away and turned toward the hospital window and gazed at the water in the distance. What was Hodgkin's disease? What kind of surgery? What was radiation therapy? What about high school—my sophomore year was starting in about two weeks?

Daddy reached out, put his hand on my shoulder and urged, "You're going to fight this thing. You're going to beat it."

I didn't know what to say. If my dad said I was going to fight, then I was going to fight, although the opponent whom I would be fighting remained amorphous. In my mind, I named it *the Beast* though I never uttered that name aloud.

⌐∽

Looking back, the strangest thing about this entire exchange when I was a teen was that no one ever used the word *cancer*. I'm not sure when I figured out that Hodgkin's disease was a type of cancer, but it wasn't during those early days. I don't think I realized

I had cancer even after I started going to Memorial Sloan Kettering in New York for treatment.

I don't know why no one told me, although it could have been a function of the times. Hodgkin's disease was what Hodgkin's lymphoma was called back then, as the pages of medical records I obtained refer to me having *Hodgkin's disease*. Also, when I was a kid, the word *cancer* was rarely uttered and spoken of only in hushed voices.

If I had to guess, I would bet that Mom persuaded Dr. Forte and Daddy not tell me that Hodgkin's disease was a type of cancer. If I had to guess, Dr. Forte and Daddy would have argued for honesty. If I had to guess, Mom's instinct to protect me from something more frightening than Hodgkin's disease won out, and Daddy and Dr. Forte went along with her.

*Or, perhaps, no one gave it any thought at all.*

⌣

Unlike then, I knew exactly what we'd be fighting now.

Tim nodded, brushed my forehead with his lips, and turned away.

"What about the kids?" I continued, "I don't want to tell Tom or James, or call Katie at college, until we know what's going on with the type of treatment I'll need."

"Let's wait until we know what's happening, so we can talk to them all at once. There's no reason to stress everyone out."

I steeled my spine and pushed the diagnosis into the darkest part of me. I knew how to organize things in neat little boxes.

I breezed into the kitchen, pulled our white china dinner plates from the cabinets, and set the table. When the family gathered for dinner, it looked like it could have been any other evening.

"Tom, have you decided what you want for your birthday dinner tomorrow night?" I asked, smiling at him. "I can't believe that you'll be fifteen tomorrow."

"Steak and chocolate cake."

"That, I can do, sweetie."

"And Mom, on Saturday, when my friends come over, can we have barbecued brisket and mac and cheese. Can you make cornbread?"

"For my favorite carnivores, of course! Who is coming over, again?" Normally able to order and organize anything, my mind had lost track of these little details, as a result of the tornado of news that had passed through.

"Joe, J.J., Steven, and Nick," Tom responded.

These boys were Tom's closest friends; they had been in and out of classes and the pool together since second grade. I loved these no-longer boys. They were not quite men, just like my own, their silhouettes slowly becoming chiseled and their voices deep and husky. They were good guys, and Tom would need them in the days to come.

"Umm, thanks, Mom," Tom offered as his blue eyes smiled at me.

As I wiped down the counters, I noticed the flickering candle mirrored in the inky windowpane. Doubt chilled my veins. *How will I hold onto the light?*

Later, Tim emerged from his office and crashed on the leather sofa in our family room. I joined him, curled under his arm. We didn't speak. What was there to say? We were in limbo, knowing the bad news, but not knowing where or how to go on from here.

⌣

Some years later, I sat at my kitchen counter exhausted from Tom's last three-day championship swim meet. I'd been a swim mom for eleven years, but his days of club swimming were now over, a bittersweet milestone.

I needed some mindless task, so I opened the junk drawer and dumped its contents onto the counter. I found three takeout chopsticks; a thirteen-year-old baby proof outlet cover; a piece to a coffee pot I no longer own; replacement bulbs for Christmas lights; a baby bottle cleaner; and three wood screws.

*Why do I hang on to this stuff? And, doesn't everyone do this? Don't we all have a place in the house for life's flotsam—picture hooks, nightlight bulbs, Scotch tape, and the other nutty things we save?*

It struck me then that knowledge about experiencing and surviving cancer is similar. Over time, from diagnosis through treatment and recovery, I accumulated my many, many experiences. These were the tools, tips, or tricks that helped me get through—the *gadgets* that worked for me.

What worked for me may or may not work for someone else. Nevertheless, I want to share them throughout this story in the hope that some practical knowledge will ease a mind, offer hope, or shine a little light along the way.

⌒

## The Practical Reality
### Communicating

My psychiatrist described getting a cancer diagnosis as standing on the edge of the ocean watching a huge wave break over me. That's because, although I knew how to swim, I couldn't handle that much water. The weight of a diagnosis is so crushing, life-altering, and terrifying that our typical, functioning selves can malfunction under the tonnage. We may forget things, get confused, or freeze, unable to process or plan our lives as we had done.

For these reasons, *take your spouse, partner, family member, or trusted friend with you to your appointments.* Ask them to take notes about *everything* the doctors or other health care professionals say. *It's important to ask questions about the diagnosis and treatment, and what it all means.* So, ask as many questions during this time as you need until you understand the explanation.

And, don't be afraid to follow-up if you have a question after your appointment. Call or text your physician instead of worrying about it or forgetting about it by the time the next appointment rolls around. I also found it helpful to keep a notebook to jot down a question or concern for my doctors whenever it popped into my head—whether it was two in the morning or while I was waiting to pick up a kid from school. Then, I'd make a list of all my questions before my next appointment and ask them.

# Chapter 2
## The Day Started Out Normal Enough

To Do (2/3)
Write president's column for PTO newsletter
Remind Tom to take water bottle to swim practice
Listen to James comment on my incessant need to over-explain
Learn new medical term, *junky*
Schedule biopsy

ONE MONTH EARLIER, LIFE was as it should've been. I'd checked a number of items off my to-do list, including the writing of the president's column for our high school PTO newsletter. I finished my coffee and enjoyed the last few moments of the morning's silence. I ran my hand through my wavy, brown hair and went upstairs to rouse the troops.

Urging Tom, our high school freshman, out of bed, as no alarm could wake him, challenged me every morning. The outline of his broad shoulders and narrow waist—his swimmer's body—filled his comforter.

Tom rolled over, groaned, groped for his wire-rimmed glasses, and yawned. He peered at me, his eyes still groggy, and headed toward the shower.

I next woke James, our fifth grader, who bounded out of bed with far too much energy for such an hour. He soon joined me in the kitchen.

I slapped breakfast on the kitchen counter, which the boys inhaled like seals snatching herring from the air. Tim kissed me goodbye.

"Well, I'm off to the salt mines," Tim said.

"Dad, you don't work in a salt mine. You don't have to keep saying that." James rolled his blue eyes.

*When did he start doing that?*

I smiled. Indeed Tim, a partner in a public accounting firm, did not work in a salt mine. Yet when the kids were little, he started saying this when he left for work. I'm sure on some days he felt like he was mining salt, with his client demands and stress from his risk management role. Unknown to us, James had believed his words. We figured this out when James brought home one of those getting to know you worksheets that teachers hand out at the beginning of the year, and James wrote that his daddy worked in a salt mine.

Wearing my suck-it-all-in jeans to minimize my middle-aged pooch and a black turtleneck sweater, I hustled the boys out the door and into my vintage, tan Volvo station wagon, *the Sherpa*, as James called it. We drove up the main street in our little town, past the colonial Presbyterian Church and six hundred-year-old white oak tree, bare in winter's chill.

I dropped the boys at their schools and drove to the radiology center at Harding for my annual mammogram. Cancer's specter always joined me on this day, although I dared not acknowledge its presence aloud. I'd put my memories of that time in a box labeled

*Hodgkin's 1981* and packed it away on a shelf in the darkest corner of my mind. I never opened it, other than to give perfunctory medical histories: *I had Hodgkin's disease, Stage II-A, in 1981. I had a splenectomy and received radiation therapy.* I didn't speak of anything else about my experience, because if I did, I would be giving power to the Beast to return one day. As long as I kept those other memories in the Box, I'd be safe.

I followed the technician down the hallway, the sound of expensive equipment humming from behind doors, to a cold and clinical room, and ran my hand over Mom's rosary, tucked in my purse. I kept her rosary after she died in 2001, ten years after my dad. I could no longer hold her hand, but I could hold her rosary.

The white mammogram machine loomed, like an oversized panini press, against the wall. Not knowing what was to come, I silently prayed, as I did every year.

*Not this year, please.*

The technician handed me a gown and stepped out. I changed and wrapped the thin cotton gown around me, ignoring the goose bumps on my pale arms.

The technician tapped on the door, stepped in, and directed me to stand in front of the machine. Asking me to lean forward, she deftly slid the gown off my right shoulder and positioned my breast on the bottom plate.

"You're going to feel a little pressure."

She lowered the upper plate, pressing my round 38Cs as flat as she could make them. "Ready?"

I nodded.

"Don't breathe."

*As if I could inhale with my breast sandwiched between two plates.*

The machine beeped and the plates released. Exhale. One image done, three to go. The technician repositioned me to take a side view of my right breast and repeated the process on the left side before I followed her to the ultrasound room.

Having an annual ultrasound added to my usual mammogram occurred a year earlier, when I learned that my then forty-eight-year-old boobs were becoming *dense*, meaning that no matter how flat the panini press squished them, it was becoming more difficult to detect abnormalities in them. I lay down on the exam table as the sonographer squeezed warm gel onto the wand. I stared at the ceiling, silently repeating the Hail Mary in my head.

The technician rolled the wand over one breast and then the other while she recorded the images on the black-and-white screen that flickered to the right of my head. Every so often, she would type something on the keyboard and move the mouse around, taking measurements with the click of a keypad.

After she finished and walked out, I sat up and pulled my mom's rosary out of my bag and continued the litany of prayers while I waited for the signal from her to get dressed. The minutes dragged as the beads passed through my fingers.

The door to the ultrasound exam room swung open. "I'm Dr. Grey," announced a woman wearing a white coat. She strode into the room, shutting the door behind her. She had short, neatly coifed hair, and as I looked at her piercing eyes, I felt a tremor in my chest as the tectonic plates far below the once solid bedrock of my life shifted.

"You've got a cyst in your right breast that looks junky to me."

The seismic energy of the words rippled through me. "*Junky*? What do you mean? That's a technical term I've never encountered," I said, pulling the thin cotton gown tightly around me, as if it would protect from what was to come.

Dr. Grey ignored my snarkiness. "A benign cyst appears as a solid black spot. Take a look at your cyst." She pointed to the image on the ultrasound. "See, it's gray, like there's some junk, like blood or calcification, floating around in it. You're going to need to have it biopsied."

"Is it breast cancer?"

"I can't tell that. That's why you need a biopsy. I can tell you, though, that most of the time, it's nothing. I'll send the report to your gynecologist."

I cringed. She'd just jinxed me with her routine answer. She didn't mean to, but she did. Perhaps, when doctors graduate from medical school or finish their residencies, they get a guidebook, or maybe they make up their own over time, *What to Say to Patients When It's Going South*. In it are phrases such as, *In 90 percent or more of the cases, it's benign*, or *There's usually no cause for concern*, or, *It wasn't like this five, ten, fifteen years ago.*

Being deeply steeped in a tannic cup of Irish Catholic fatalism—no sugar added—I always knew I was doomed when I heard a platitude like that. Or, as one of my equally fatalistic friends explained when I asked her why she'd never told me about her parents' divorce years earlier, "I thought if I believed in a good outcome, there'd be one, and if I talked about it, this good outcome would be ruined." This was how our magical thinking worked.

I knew, with cold certainty it wouldn't be *nothing*, just like I knew it wouldn't be *nothing* all those years ago.

⌐⌐

On weekends in the seventies and early eighties, Mom, Daddy, my brother, Marty, my sister, Jenny, and I visited my aunt and uncle in Long Island, to escape Staten Island's sweltering summer heat. My relatives lived along a canal with a dock, in the little cape house and garage my uncle had built by hand after World War II.

As a child, Aunt Mary and Uncle Norman's waterfront home was a special place to me, with a deep, velvety lawn that tickled the toes, an exquisite English rose garden, and an orderly vegetable patch from which my siblings and I picked tomatoes, beans, and cucumbers.

My father taught us all to swim and to dive there. We also learned to fish, row, sail, and name the constellations from this special place. Uncle Norman crafted toy boats for us, along with a rowboat for my brother, on a workbench organized with military precision. "A place for everything, and everything in its place," he would say.

Aunt Mary, diminutive with bright blue eyes and never without her deep red lipstick, was like a fairy godmother. She'd say things like, "We should be free. You should come live on a houseboat with us and stay home from school." On rainy afternoons, I played with her old manual Smith Corona typewriter from her days working in a typing pool. The ancient machine had round keys and a satisfying bell that signaled the end of a line. I wrote stories sitting cross-legged in the garage attic and listening to the steady patter of a summer storm. On the beautiful days, I spent hours reading in the sun on the far end of the dock, turning a shade of crimson that matched my red polka dot swimsuit.

One August weekend when I was a few months shy of my fifteenth birthday, I again spent the day reading and sunning. I stood and stretched, only after my mom called me to help with dinner.

I was walking toward my aunt's house when Jenny ran up behind me, threw her arm around my neck, and hugged me, her still damp bathing suit grazing my sizzling back.

"Ouch. You idiot. What are you doing?" I demanded with all the scorn a teenage girl could direct at her annoying younger sister.

"Chris, you have a big bump on your neck," Jenny said, pointing to the spot that was smarting from her hug, "Mommy needs to look at that. Hey, Mom, you need to look at Chris's neck!!"

"What are you talking about, Jenny?" Mom asked.

"Yeah, what are you talking about? There's nothing wrong with my neck."

"Yes, there is," Jenny insisted, pulling me by my arm until I was standing in front of Mom. Jenny poked at the right side of my neck. "Look, Mom, it's all swollen."

"Would you quit it?" I said, brushing her hand away.

Mom got up and walked over to where I stood. She was five feet, eleven inches tall, with thick, brown, wavy hair, and a nurse.

She had trained at St. Vincent's Nursing School in New York in the early 1960s and worked on medical and surgical floors at New York hospitals and later in nursing homes. Mom didn't mess around.

She examined the bump and then ran her fingers around my neck, like she always did when I had a cold or a sore throat. Her lips formed a thin line, her brows furrowed, and her face shifted from Mom on a Saturday in the summer sun, to her commanding and professional face.

⌣

Years later my sister explained Mom's change in face to me.

"She was afraid, Chris. She also probably thought that she should've caught it. You'd lost weight. You didn't seem like yourself. Or maybe she saw the symptoms and was in denial about them. Either way, she was probably feeling guilty, so she went into nurse mode and shut down."

I must've registered Mom's fear, at least subconsciously, but I wouldn't have asked how she felt at the time. Mom didn't discuss feelings, hers or anyone else's. She'd never admit to fear—that could cause us pain. Yet in that momentary transformation from mom to nurse, my mother showed me all I needed to know about how I'd handle whatever was to come.

I'd never speak of my fear. I'd place it neatly to one side of the shelves on which I'd order my life going forward.

⌣

"I think we'll have that looked at by a doctor on Monday," Mom pronounced.

"Do I have to go to the doctor? I'm fine," I whined, trying to keep the fear of the unknown out of my voice, "Couldn't it be a pulled muscle or something?"

"I'm not sure. That's why we'll go to the doctor on Monday. Now, please go help your aunt with dinner."

"But, Mom..."

My voice trailed off as she raised her eyebrows. Her hazel eyes signaled that the conversation was over. I understood exactly what she expected of me: I would do what I was told.

"Thanks a lot, Jenny," I sniped as I stomped off to help my aunt.

⌣

I should have thanked my sister. Mom always called my sister the *observant* one. So, I should have thanked her with some measure of sincerity because she helped save my life on that summer day. Not surprisingly, Jenny followed in our mother's footsteps and became a nurse.

⌣

Years later, I knew what news a biopsy could bring.

"Please guide me on whatever path is before me. Please give me strength to walk it because I'm going to need it," I whispered as I put the rosary in my purse. As I stood in the ultrasound room, alone with my unspoken memories and the ghosts of cancer past, I broke down.

*I'm too young. I want to see Katie, Tom, and James grow up and start their lives and families. And Tim—I can't imagine him alone for the next thirty-plus years.*

I loved my over-scheduled life, my family, and my friends. I loved being involved in the school community. I loved organizing Tom's club and high school swim team banquets, having our home filled with swimmers during team pasta parties and going to his meets. I loved visiting Katie at college, taking her and her friends out to dinner, and hearing them talk about their classes, professors, and parties, their own lives beginning to take shape. I loved watching James run cross-country and cheering for him as he breezed by.

My deepest fear—that one day I'd face the Beast again—paralyzed me. *I can hear its footsteps and feel its hand swiping at me as I tried to stay out of reach. How much longer can I outpace it?*

After a few more minutes, I wiped away my tears, blew my nose, and walked out of the radiology center. Maybe I'd get lucky this time. Maybe it would be nothing. I debated whether I should call Tim with my mammogram and ultrasound results but decided against it. I didn't want him to worry all day.

Hours later, when the day's comings and goings, work and meetings, homework and swim practice were done, Tim and I finally sunk into the tan leather sofa in the family room for our nightly hour after the boys had retreated to their rooms. Tim stretched out in his jeans and favorite flannel shirt, with the TV controller in his hand. I curled up at the other end in my favorite running tights and long-sleeved tee shirt, with my book. The big screen TV flickered mutely on the cream-colored wall in front of us.

As Tim scanned the channels, I put my book in my lap and brought up what I'd been avoiding telling him all day.

"So, I had my annual mammogram and ultrasound this morning."

Tim sat up, put the controller down and leaned in. "I'm sorry. I totally forgot. Why didn't you call me when it was over? Is everything okay?"

"I didn't call you because it didn't go as well as I would have liked. The radiologist said I have a *junky* cyst in my right breast that needs to be biopsied."

The color drained from Tim's face, and he placed his head in his hands for a moment. "What the hell does that mean?" Tim exclaimed when he looked up, his voice agitated.

"Can we not panic? Please, sweetie," I urged, trying to conceal the worry in my voice. Repeating what the radiologist told me and lowering my voice, I continued, "There was some junk, like blood or something, in the cyst. Most of the time, it's nothing to worry about."

Tim cocked one eye at me.

"She's going to send the report to my gynecologist. He'll refer me to a breast surgeon. I'll make the appointment for the biopsy once I hear from him. It could take a couple of weeks."

Tim looked at me, his faced lined with worry. I took both his hands in mine.

"Listen to me," I urged. In my most measured tone I continued, "We've been down this road before. I have. You have, with your dad. We'll take everything one step at a time."

"Yeah, but look what happened to him!"

"And look what happened to *me*. I'm not going anywhere, except to bed."

I smiled at Tim and nodded my head in the direction of the stairs. I needed the warmth of his arms, comfort, and love that night.

⁓

A few days later, my gynecologist called.

"I looked at your mammogram and ultrasound results, Chris. I want you to call Dr. Diehl to schedule a biopsy. He's the best. If my wife needed a breast biopsy, I'd send her to him," he said.

I believed him but I still ran my own background check on Dr. Diehl. I reached out to several friends who'd had breast cancer and found out two of them had used him for their breast surgeries and loved him. Not only was he an excellent surgeon—precise and detail-oriented, they told me—but also kind, gentle, and had a great bedside manner. That was good enough for me.

I scheduled the biopsy for the end of February, almost a month away, and tried to put it out of my mind.

# Chapter 3
## The Waiting Really is the Hardest Part

To Do (2/29)
Have biopsy
Wait

As I drove to Dr. Diehl's office for the biopsy, I couldn't help but think how differently cancer was diagnosed today as compared to the way it was in 1981. I knew my biopsy with Dr. Diehl would take about a half-hour, unlike in the eighties when, as a fourteen-year-old, I spent two weeks in the hospital having surgeries and waiting to learn what would happen to me.

Mom and Daddy drove me home from Long Island on that hot Sunday afternoon in August, and my siblings stayed with my aunt and uncle. My parents must have asked my aunt and uncle if Jenny and Marty could stay with them. That thought never entered my mind, though. I assumed they wanted to spend some more time lazing away summer's last days in Long Island and had asked to stay.

But years later, Jenny told me how she frightened she was when my parents left with me in the backseat of the car because she knew something was wrong. She felt abandoned.

When Jenny mentioned this to me, I reacted with surprise and some anger. *What could she have been afraid of? The fear belonged to me. I own it and kept it packed safely in the dark. Besides, she wasn't the one who had had the mystery bump on her neck.*

As I reflected, however, I realized that of course Jenny had been afraid. She'd found the bump. She'd seen how upset Mom was. She was afraid that something bad would happen to her older sister.

*How could I have missed that?*

But I did, for thirty-five years. I'm not proud of that.

⟵⟶

On Monday morning, my dad took me to Staten Island Hospital—where he was the director of Human Resources—so I could meet with whatever doctor my dad asked to see me. I assumed that once the doctor took a look at me, I'd find out I was fine and spend the rest of the day volunteering with one of my high school friends, Trina—like normal.

In short order, a burly man, a little taller than my dad, walked into my father's office. His voice boomed as he greeted my dad and me.

"Hi, Marty, and hello there, kiddo. I'm Dr. Forte. Can I look at your neck?"

He smiled at me, his rich, dark eyes dancing behind his glasses, as I nodded. He pressed his fingers into the bump on my neck, doing the same thing Mom had done.

"Does that hurt?" he asked.

"Nope."

Dr. Forte then started speaking in that slow, measured voice doctors use when they're about to say something unpleasant, like "Oh, this won't hurt a bit," or "It'll just be a little prick," when that was not at all what was coming.

"I want to ask you some questions. Have you felt really tired lately?"

I paused, not knowing that I was beginning the first of many rounds of what I came to call, the *question game*.

"I'm on summer vacation, so not really. Not like during school."

"Are you tired during school?"

"Yeah, I have to get up early," I replied, trying to figure out why it mattered if I was tired.

"I mean, do you feel tired when you haven't done anything that would normally make you feel tired?"

There was that time a month or so before, when I helped Aunt Anne clean her apartment. I felt exhausted after doing that.

"No, I don't think so," I answered.

I didn't like this questioning. Dr. Forte must have thought something was wrong with me.

"Have you woken up at night and been hot or sweaty?"

"Well, we don't have air-conditioning in my room, and it is summer. My room is warm, but I have a fan." I replied, hoping that the question game would end soon.

"Have you noticed that maybe your pajamas were wet when you woke up?"

My stomach froze. At the beginning of the summer, my friends and I had a slumber party. When I woke up, I noticed my top was soaking wet with sweat. I felt cold and clammy then—and now I was getting the same feeling as I stood in front of Dr. Forte.

"I, uh, don't remember."

I hoped my face didn't give me away although I'm sure it did— I've never had a poker face.

Dr. Forte raised his eyes and asked again, "Are you sure?"

I knew he knew I was lying, but I couldn't admit that I was in front of my dad.

"I really don't remember."

Dr. Forte's eyes revealed his disappointment in my response. He changed his tack, told me that he wanted me to have a chest x-ray and some blood tests.

*Tests that wouldn't lie,* I thought with embarrassment.

⌒

*Why didn't I tell Dr. Forte the truth?*

I must have thought if I told him that I'd been unusually tired or woken up soaked with sweat, something was really wrong. I also knew in my gut that something *was* really wrong. And I couldn't talk about how afraid I was because my mom had made clear that we didn't discuss such things. Rather than confront the truth that was staring me in the face, I steadfastly maintained that I was *fine* in the hope that I would be.

I imagine Dr. Forte must've understood how terrified I was. He must've known that I'd need to buy into whatever was in front of me. So, perhaps that's why he didn't call me out in front of my dad.

⌒

Some hours later, Dr. Forte met with my parents and me in my father's office and sat down next to me in a chair across from my dad's desk. He got right down to business.

"Kiddo, I've taken a look at your x-rays and tests, and I want you to have something called a biopsy to tell us what's wrong."

"Isn't that what the x-rays and blood tests were supposed to do?" I snapped, forgetting my manners, and tired from all the tests and stress-inducing questions. "Don't you know what's wrong with me? What's a biopsy, anyway?"

My mom gave me a sharp look.

Dr. Forte continued in his slow, serious doctor voice. "The other tests have given me an idea. A biopsy is a small operation that will give me more information about what might be wrong."

"Operation. I'm not having any operation. You can forget that!" I exclaimed.

"Do you trust me, kiddo?" Dr. Forte asked.

The question was ridiculous. Of course, I trusted him. He was a doctor, after all, and my parents wouldn't have let him take care of me if they didn't know and trust him. I knew he wanted to find out what was wrong and help me. I nodded.

"Okay, so here's what will happen," Dr. Forte continued calmly and firmly. "You're going to stay in the hospital for a few days. On the day of the biopsy, which I'm trying to schedule right now, you're going to be given medicine to make you sleep, and another doctor is going to make a tiny cut where that bump on your neck is, to take some tissue out of it. It's not going to hurt. Then, you'll wake up."

"I don't want to stay in the hospital by myself. I want to go home."

I turned and looked at Daddy, who opened his arms. I went right into them. My tears ran onto his blue button-down shirt that held a trace of his spicy cologne. Mom stood and wrapped her arms across my back, so I was sandwiched between them.

"Shh, it's going to be okay," my dad said, stroking my hair and lifting my chin up so I would look at him. "You get to be a patient in my hospital. You can tell me whether everyone's doing a good job, okay?"

Nodding, I croaked, "Okay."

"I'll run home and get your clothes, toothbrush, and whatever else you want," Mom said.

"And some books too? Please."

❧

From the moment I first understood that *Jane and Dick* were running as I turned the pages of those early readers, books have been my companions. I remember the magic of figuring out that all those letters meant something, and a door to the world opened to me. I spent summers sitting in the New York Public Library in the St. George section of Staten Island and in the bookmobile that would visit our neighborhood every week. From *Madeline*, to *Blueberries for Sal*, to Beverley Cleary's *Ramona* books, to Laura Ingalls Wilder's *Little House on the Prairie*, to *The Secret Garden* and *The Little Princess*, and every Judy Blume book, I read everything I could and more. So, I couldn't imagine spending any time in a hospital without some books to keep me company.

⌢

By the end of the day, I had an ID band on my wrist and was sitting in a bed in the bright yellow pediatric unit. I had my own room, and the window looked out over Seaview Avenue east toward the water. If I stretched looking out on an angle, I could see the Verrazano Bridge in the distance. After my mom and dad left, I fell asleep. I awoke with a start, when I heard a voice.

"Hey there, kiddo. How are you doing?" Dr. Forte was standing at the foot of my bed. "I wanted to check on you before I left."

I sat up, rubbing the sleep from my eyes, then pushed on my glasses. Dr. Forte looked more rumpled than he was earlier that morning. He'd loosened his tie and his hair looked like he had run his hands through it a bunch of times. I looked out the window before I answered. The streetlights' halo of light flickered over Seaview Avenue, while the red taillights of the cars cruising down Father Capodanno Boulevard glinted in the distance—an ordinary hot summer night on Staten Island.

"Oh, Dr. Forte. What are you still doing here? It's dark out. Shouldn't you go home? My parents left a while ago. I guess I'm fine. I must've dozed off."

He smiled, ignoring my stream of questions.

"Good. Well, I think the biopsy will be the day after tomorrow. Eat some dinner. They left a tray for you. I'll be in to see you in the morning."

He turned to leave.

"Dr. Forte, am I going to be okay?" I asked in a polite tone, trying in my fourteen-year-old way to make a peace offering for my earlier bratty behavior.

The doctor turned back to look me. "Kiddo, I will do everything in my power to make sure you're okay, but you're going to have listen to me, be honest with me, and do what I ask you to do. Do we have a deal?"

I knew he was calling me out on my dishonesty that morning, but I liked that he didn't try to appease me or make promises he couldn't keep. At that moment, Dr. Forte made me feel cared for. I'd do whatever he told me to do even if I didn't like it and was afraid. I looked him straight in the eyes and said, "Deal."

"You sound like your dad," Dr. Forte laughed. "I'll see you tomorrow. Be good, kiddo."

A few days later on the morning of my biopsy, the day started early with a flurry of activity. A nurse started an IV for fluid and medicine that would make me sleepy. My mom arrived and sat holding my hand until the transporter came to wheel me to the operating room. My mom walked there alongside me, and when we got to the doors to the operating rooms, she squeezed my hand and said that she would see me when I woke up.

I was wheeled into the operating room and looked up at two doctors wearing green scrubs and masks and nurses moving around the room. I saw a bright light above me and stainless steel trays and equipment in the room. I wanted to look at all of it, but then one of the doctors told me that he would give me some medicine to make me fall asleep. He asked me to count back from ten. I remembered counting ten, ni—and then, black.

The next thing I remembered was cold air blowing in my face. I kept trying to brush away this source of annoyance, but every time

I reached my hand toward my face, another hand firmly pushed my hand down. I heard my name, *Christine*, seemingly shouted from another room, and an instruction that I needed to leave the mask on my face because I needed the oxygen to wake up.

Wake up? I didn't want to wake up. I was comfy being asleep.

"Don't you want to see your mom, Christine?" the disembodied voice asked. "She's waiting to see you, but you have to wake up."

I did want to see my mom. I was sure of that, so I opened my eyes, squinting at the bright lights, and saw a nurse standing by my bed. I learned that the operation was over, and I was in the recovery room.

"As soon as you sit up and have some ice, your mom can come in," the nurse told me.

Ice sounded appealing. My mouth was dry, and my throat was really sore. The nurse told me to only have a few chips to start because I might feel queasy from the anesthesia.

A few minutes passed, and my mom came in. She looked tired, and her eyes were red. She sat down on the small chair next to my bed and slipped the rosary wrapped around her fingers into her purse.

"How are you, pumpkin?" she asked as she ran her hand across my forehead.

"I think okay," I croaked.

"Don't try to talk too much. Your throat is sore from the anesthesia."

She fed me ice chips and said that the operation went well. She walked alongside the stretcher as I was wheeled back to my room.

It was mid-afternoon by the time I got resettled. There were vases of white daisies, little yellow roses, and pink carnations lining the windowsill from my aunts and grandma. My neck was sore, so the nurses brought me some pain medication, but that made me sick. My mom stayed with me as I dozed on and off for the rest of the afternoon. My dad came up from his office to check on me and told me how proud he was of me for being brave.

I didn't feel brave at all, especially after my mom and dad left.

I didn't appreciate how extraordinary, how unusual my path from ordinary teen to cancer patient was. Having now spent more than my fair share of time with doctors and in hospitals, I knew how many hours were spent waiting for appointments, referrals, insurance approvals, follow-up appointments, tests, and results. Waiting for a plan. Yet, as a fourteen-year-old with a mysterious bump on her neck, I didn't have to wait at all. Even though he worked at the hospital, my father still must have moved heaven and earth to have me seen, admitted, and treated as quickly as I'd been.

Thirty-five years later, I didn't need to be admitted to a hospital to have a breast biopsy. Dr. Diehl entered the exam room in his office where I was waiting and holding the same rosary that my mom had once held.

He was tall and fit, wearing a crisp blue-striped oxford, tie, and navy dress slacks under his pristine white lab coat. I found his meticulous manner and calm voice reassuring, as he explained the procedure step by step: a local anesthetic, a needle aspiration, a marker inserter at the biopsy site. *Done.*

Then, as Dr. Diehl applied the dressings, he too unwittingly called the Fates down on my head.

"Chris, ninety-five percent of the time, these cysts are benign. So, don't worry. I'll call you as soon as I have the results, in a couple of days."

My heart skipped a beat when I heard those words. I wanted to believe him. I wanted to be in the ninety-five percent. I pushed my fear into the Box and prayed that the Beast would stay there.

# Chapter 4
## Does Anyone Know Where We're Going?

To Do (3/3 to 3/7)
Stop sleeping
Pray
P/up steaks and birthday cake
Schedule MRI
Schedule ultrasound
Schedule appointment with oncologist
Call Athena
Panic
Xanax
Sleep

I PICKED UP MY phone off the bedside table, checking the time again. This time, it glowed 2:30 a.m. The *what if* conversations played in an endless loop in my head. Sleep eluded me this night and would for many more.

*What if I die?*

*You're not going to die from this.*

*I could, though. If I die, Tim has to get remarried. He'd never function without a wife. I'll have to talk to him about this. Who would he marry? What would the kids think?*

*You don't need to think about that at all, Christine, since you are not going to die, and Tim isn't getting remarried.*

*I guess the boobs need to go.*

*That's extreme since you don't know what you're dealing with yet.*

*No, they're both going. I'm doing this once. That's it. But what if I have to have chemo?*

*You'll deal with it.*

*I don't want to have chemo.*

*You don't have much of a choice if that's what the doctors tell you.*

*What if I lose my hair?*

*Then, you'll be bald.*

*You're not helping.*

*You started it. You know what you should do right now?*

*What?*

*Stop. Go to sleep. Say a Hail Mary and go to sleep.*

*Okay, but I won't wear those ugly turban things if I lose my hair.*

My mind circled around these questions until I finally said a Hail Mary, Mom's go-to answer for most of life's problems. *Can't sleep? Say a Hail Mary. Worried about a test in school? Say a Hail Mary. See an ambulance or a hearse go by, say a Hail Mary.*

I said a Hail Mary and drifted into a fitful sleep.

⌒

Tom's fifteenth birthday dawned. I spent the morning filling up my calendar, not with things I wanted to do, but with things my doctors wanted me to do, making appointment after appointment for the following week. I also had to take Tom to Lancaster, Pennsylvania to his state championship swim meet later that same week. I didn't know how I'd keep it together.

I knew Tim and the kids would always be there for me. But, my family isn't always the best in a crisis—not due to a lack of love, but perhaps, too much. The fear of loss paralyzes our thoughts; our emotions cloud our judgment. I knew how terrified Tim was, and I didn't want to add to his anxiety and fear of all things medical by piling on mine.

So, I turned to my girlfriends—the ones who would prop me up when I couldn't lean on my family. My girlfriends would help get me through, and as I learned months later, would help get Tim through, too. I didn't want to tell a lot of people what was going on before Tim and I spoke to the kids, but certain people had to know, like the kids' school counselors, my fellow board members of the high school parent-teacher organization, and Joanne, the president of the swim team parents' organization for Tom's team. I was running the annual team banquet—only a month away and with many tasks to do. What if I couldn't do it all? I knew Joanne would understand. She'd had breast cancer. But I couldn't think about these conversations now.

More than anyone else, I needed to talk to Athena. Dark-haired, fiercely loyal, and with a wicked sense of humor, Athena was from Taiwan and immigrated to the U.S. in 1976 when she was thirteen. Athena and I became friends in 2008 when we joined a new multi-sport club at our local YMCA and started training for and competing in triathlons.

In 2009, Athena developed a severe infection in her hand and arm that almost killed her. She needed surgery, skin grafts, and months of rehabilitation. All of her tri-buddies came to her aid, visiting her in the hospital, making meals, picking up kids, and driving her to appointments. Following a long recovery, Athena made her way back to the pool, got back on her bike, and started running again.

Athena and I grew even closer once her three boys started swimming competitively along with my daughter and older son. We saw each other at meets almost every weekend during the season. She was one of my dear ones, those whom I hold closest in my heart.

I collapsed into my favorite comfy, creamy-colored chair in the corner of the family room and called Athena, who worked as a physician assistant at a cancer center. She dealt with cancer patients every day, but more importantly, Athena was no stranger to medical crises, having had her own.

"Hey, Athena, can you talk?" I asked and blurted, "I got my biopsy results. It's breast cancer, lucky me, or as you folks call it, *invasive ductal carcinoma*. It's small, and they caught it early."

"Did your doc tell you what stage? Or the size or grade?" Athena quickly asked in her clipped, professional manner.

"Stage one, I think. I don't know the size or grade. I don't have the report yet. They have to run more pathology tests to determine the exact flavor of breast cancer. They said it'll take a week or so before I'll know."

"It will. Those additional tests will tell you whether you are estrogen receptor or progesterone receptor, positive or negative, and whether you are human epidermal growth factor receptor 2 or HER2, positive or negative. That will determine whether you'll need chemotherapy, surgery, or radiation."

"In English, please."

In a mini-biology lesson, Athena explained that *receptors* are proteins on the surface of certain cells. Receptors act like switches; when they are turned on, they tell the cell to do something. When they worked like they are supposed to, cells are healthy and happy. When they don't work, shit happens, like cancer. The different therapies work to shut down the malfunctioning switches, like cutting a fuel line to an engine, then the problem cells die.

"So, the report I'm waiting for will tell me if I need chemotherapy or surgery or both."

"You might also need radiation."

"I don't think I can have radiation since I had Hodgkin's. I'm sure that was a one-shot deal. I hope I don't need chemo," I sighed. "That's the last thing I want to go through. I scheduled a breast MRI for Monday and an ultrasound on Thursday."

"I can come with you to the MRI, if you want." Athena offered.

Brushing her off, I responded, "No. You don't need to blow part of your day sitting with me while I get an MRI. I'll be fine, but thanks."

I was wrong about that. Would it have killed me to say, *Yes, Athena, please come with me?* She was a physician assistant. She knew more about MRIs than I did. She must have offered me the support because she thought I'd need it.

Why did I have this incessant need to do it all on my own?

⌒

I knew exactly why: my parents expected I'd do what they asked me, when they asked me, and that whatever task would be done right. They worked long hours, and when my father was in contract negotiations, he was absent from home for weeks at time. My mom typically worked the night and evening shifts, and there were plenty of holidays and birthdays when she had to work. Mom expected that the three of us, led by me, would help around the house. So Mom taught us how to clean *correctly*, meaning everything was disinfected and damn close to sterile. She taught us how to set a table, complete with napkin rings and candles, and how to make beds with perfect hospital corners at right angles, tucked and tight. She taught us how to clean a skinned knee and that warm salt water is the answer to many of life's ailments.

Daddy taught us how to hold and use a kitchen knife so we wouldn't require first aid. He taught us how to dice an onion, to scramble the perfect egg, and to make his mother's Thanksgiving stuffing. He and my mom also made us to learn things on our own. If we didn't understand a word we read and asked for help, they'd point to the huge *Random House Unabridged Dictionary* on the bookshelf and say, "Look it up."

My siblings and I all learned these things, but I insisted on doing them so when my parents came home from work, they'd find a clean house, where the beds were made and the table set correctly. I didn't trust my brother and sister to help because they were younger, and I never wanted to hear that something hadn't met my parents' standards.

I was afraid of making mistakes. I thought if I did the chores myself, my parents wouldn't be disappointed or worse, angry, because I'd done something wrong.

⌣

Continuing to offer me advice, Athena said, "One more thing, Chris, stay off the Internet. There's too much information out there, and most of it's crap. If you insist on looking, which I know you'll do, look at good sites, like Memorial Sloan Kettering's, the National Cancer Institute, or breastcancer.org."

"Okay, okay. I will. Thanks, Athena."

A few minutes later, Athena texted: *I'm sorry if I came off sounding too impersonal. Sometimes, I get too clinical, and I didn't mean to sound like I don't care.*

*If I wanted a cookie, I'd go to a bakery*, I responded.

I was okay with Athena being clinical and objective because it's what I needed. And, as my journey progressed, I would lean on Athena over and over. When I felt like my world was spiraling out of control, Athena was a calm, authoritative voice. I trusted her opinion and judgment.

⌣

Over the following months, I followed Athena's guidance, avoiding almost all the cancer-related websites except reputable, established sources (see *Resources*), such as the National Cancer

Institute (cancer.gov) and breastcancer.org, which I visited repeatedly. I found breastcancer.org easy to navigate. Finding a research topic was easy. The articles were written well and provided information without being scary. The site gave me questions to ask my doctors and nurses and answered my questions between appointments.

⌒

After speaking with Athena about my results, I headed out to pick up Tom's birthday dinner so we could celebrate something. That evening, in the warmth of our kitchen, Tim and I, and the boys, sat together at our family table and feasted on a perfectly grilled ribeye. We sang *Happy Birthday* and enjoyed slices of rich chocolate cake. Tom opened his gifts and liked his new headphones, video games, and sweater. Katie called from college to wish Tom a happy birthday. We celebrated a normal at-home birthday party.

Check.

*How many more would we have?*

⌒

I filled the next few days with *normal*. Tom had another swim meet over the weekend, and we had his friends over for a birthday sleepover, complete with pulled pork, barbecued ribs, coleslaw, and macaroni and cheese. The boys devoured everything and stayed up all night playing *Diablo III*. Hearing the sound of their laughter and shouts from our den as I drifted off to sleep made me smile. I'd given Tom this night with his friends—a normal teenage night.

Before I knew it, it was Monday, MRI day. I'd had multiple CT scans and they never bothered me. How bad could an MRI be? I should have known something was up when the nurse asked me if I'd ever had an MRI before and seemed surprised I hadn't and was alone.

"MRIs are very loud. I'm not sure if you're aware," the nurse said.

"We'll give you noise reduction headphones. I can program music for you. What type of music do you like?"

"No, I wasn't aware, but I like Stevie Nicks, Steely Dan, the Pretenders . . ." She looked at me as if she had no idea who these performers were.

I climbed onto the table and lay face down with arms at my sides. My breasts were positioned in cutouts on the table and sandwiched in between plates like during a mini-mammogram. The nurse put the headphones over my ears, as I was thoroughly immobilized at that point. The earphones buzzed to life like a mission control center from outer space.

"Hi, Mrs. Corrigan," the technician said into my ear. "I'll be doing your MRI today. Each image will take two to five minutes. I'll let you know when each one will start. The whole MRI should take about 45 minutes. It's important that you not move, okay? We'll start the music soon."

*How on earth could I possibly move? My boobs are between two vice grips.*

"We're going to start; the first image is about two minutes."

Imagine, for a moment, that your body has been placed inside a large bell and an entire crew of construction workers is standing outside the bell hitting it with sledgehammers. That noise would be whisper-like compared to the ungodly, nerve-shattering, bone-rattling clanking and banging of an MRI.

The headphones sputtered. Over the MRI's awful noise, my brain slowly began to register the strains of one of my favorite Fleetwood Mac ballads, *Landslide*, sung by Stevie Nicks.

On any other day, I would have enjoyed hearing *Landslide*, but not on this day. Listening to Stevie sing about love and loss, aging and children, my fears of cancer, of death, of losing all the people I loved the most, overwhelmed me. Why did Pandora pick this song? Why not *My Old School* or *Gypsy* or *Back on the Chain Gang*?

Tears started streaming down my face; snot ran from my nose. I couldn't breathe. I started shaking.

"Mrs. Corrigan, are you okay?" the headphones crackled. "Would you like me to send the nurse in to sit with you? You can't move. The next study is five minutes."

"No, I'm not okay. I'm anything but okay," I cried. "Can you please send the nurse in?"

I began to hear Pink Floyd's *Comfortably Numb*, the irony of which was overwhelming, and begged, "Please, no more music."

The nurse came in, sat down next to me, and held my hand for the next forty minutes. I was grateful to have someone sit with me, to remind me to breathe, and to help keep the panic at bay.

Finally, the MRI ended, and I apologized to the nurse and technician.

"I don't know what happened to me. I don't normally get claustrophobic or panic-attacks, but that was horrible."

"You did fine. Don't worry about it."

I found out later that the MRI report noted: "Patient was reportedly claustrophobic. There is some motion on this study, which does degrade imaging."

My MRI experience was a far cry from my memory of my first CT scan, which I had shortly before I started radiation therapy in September of 1981.

⌒

I was alone in the imaging room, for no one else was allowed in there—other than for the technician, of course. There was no kindness offered there, either: I remember being sternly lectured to not move *for any reason,* or I'd have to come back for another scan and if that happened, all my treatment would be delayed.

It was freezing cold lying on the hard table during the scanning process, and I kept trying not to shiver. I was terrified that I'd mess up and be in a ton of trouble.

When the scan finally ended, the technician sent me to get dressed, and I met Mom in the waiting room.

"Hi, the tech told me what a great job you did. I know it was hard, and I'm proud of you."

"Thanks, Mommy," I replied, so relieved that I didn't make a mistake.

I didn't tell her how scared and cold I was, or how unpleasant the technician had seemed to me. Then, I'd be complaining or, worse, admitting my fear.

I pushed all of those unspoken feelings down into the dark, down into the Box.

⌒

A few hours later, I dropped off Tom at swim practice. My cell phone rang as he stepped out the car and shut the door.

"Hi, Dr. Diehl. I wasn't expecting to hear from you today."

"I got the MRI report and wanted to talk to you. Well, Chris, the good news is it doesn't appear that there is any cancer in your axillary nodes. There is a small satellite spot next to the original tumor site, and there are indeterminate spots in the left breast we'll need to take a look at on the ultrasound that's scheduled for Thursday."

I started shaking—this time, hyperventilating—which was strange since Dr. Diehl was giving me good news. The strain of the past five days since I got my biopsy results was catching up with me.

"Dr. Diehl, I cannot do this," I stammered. "I can't think. I can't sleep. I can't breathe. This never happens to me, but I simply can't deal with it all," I hiccupped.

"I want you to take a deep breath, hold it, and let it out. Then, do it again," Dr. Diehl instructed.

We were silent as I tried to get my breathing under control.

"How are you doing?" he asked.

"Better." My heart had stopped racing.

"Listen, Chris, you're going through a lot, more than most people have to go through. I'll prescribe you something so that you can sleep. You need to sleep. One more thing, you call me any time you need. Okay?"

"Okay, thanks."

I ended the call, drove straight to my pharmacy, and picked up a prescription for Xanax. I'd never taken it before, but that night I was finally able to sleep with no conversations in my head. I woke up the next morning feeling rested for the first time in many days.

Check.

# Chapter 5
## The Best Laid Plans

To Do (3/8 to 3/10)
Meet Joanne for coffee
Pick up snacks for Tom
Ultrasound
Get pathology report
States in Lancaster

I TRIED TO FILL up the next few days so I wouldn't think about the ultrasound and the pending pathology report.

On Tuesday morning, I met Joanne, the swim team parents' organization president, at Starbucks and told her about my diagnosis. The comforting scent of freshly roasted and brewed coffee and the ubiquitous jazzy music emanating from the speakers overhead were incongruous with my news.

"Oh, Chris. I'm sorry," Joanne whispered, almost choking on the words. Her blue eyes were filled with kindness.

I rummaged through my bag for a tissue.

"I'm sorry," I said, wiping my eyes. "I had cancer when I was a teenager, and I've always been terrified it would come back and now it has."

"Chris, I had no idea."

"I don't like to talk about it. I was fourteen when I was diagnosed with Hodgkin's lymphoma. I had surgery and three months of radiation therapy. I tried to put everything behind me, but it's probably the reason I have breast cancer now, although I never thought it would actually happen to me."

Joanne reached across the café table and gave my hand a squeeze. Then she quietly shared when she was first diagnosed, she had a lumpectomy and radiation. The cancer went into remission, and she was fine for several years. Then, it came back. She knew exactly how I felt.

"That was the worst," she confided. "It was hard on the kids to go through it twice. The second time around I had the bilateral mastectomy and reconstruction. The reconstruction was difficult because my skin was damaged from the radiation. If I had to do it all over again, I would have had the bilateral mastectomy from the beginning."

"That's the way I'm leaning, even though I'm not sure if there's cancer on the left side. I'm so stressed now, I can't imagine how I would be if it came back a third time."

"Did you tell the kids yet?"

"No. Katie knows that I had the biopsy, but I haven't told her the results because I'm waiting for the pathology report, which will determine the type of treatment I'll have. I'd rather tell the kids everything all at once, you know? I don't want to call her and tell her, 'Hey, I've got breast cancer, but I don't know how it'll be treated.' Also, I don't want this to mess with Tom's head before the state meet later this week."

"I completely understand. You don't want to do that to him."

"Tim and I want to tell them after the meet because I should know the whole story by then, and Katie's coming home from college for the weekend. So, Sunday is it."

"That's what we did with our kids. We told them at the same time."

"It makes sense, right? I want everyone on the same page, and we can all be upset together."

Joanne nodded.

I paused and pushed down the lump in my throat. "Was it terrible telling them, Joanne? I'm sick over it. I'm worried about how Katie will handle her classes, knowing I've got cancer. And the boys have all their activities. I don't know how I'm going to manage."

I searched for another tissue and blew my nose.

"It was tough to tell them, especially the second time around. My younger daughter had the hardest time, but we got through it. You will too because you're going to ask for help. Just ask. There are so many people who'll help you, Chris. I was amazed at how many people helped me—even those I never expected."

"I don't want to tell a lot of people right now."

"I get it, and I won't say anything. I kept things quiet, too, at the beginning."

In August 1981, the afternoons I was spending waiting for surgery in the hospital dragged, like the endless last class of our high school day. The business of the morning—the nurses and doctors checking in, the blood tests and breakfast tray—gave way to hours of quiet emptiness, broken only by the bleating loudspeaker.

I had my books and my hooked rug craft kit to keep me busy, but I could only read so many chapters or add so many rows to the rug. The color television on the wall softly babbled, but I only half-listened. I often gazed out the window and wondered what was going on out there in the real world, wanting to be a part of it, not stuck in a hospital bed uncertain about what would happen next. The only cure for such boredom was sleep, and I dozed most afternoons.

One day, sensing a presence in my room, I opened my eyes to see Trina, my high school buddy, walking toward me.

"Oh my gosh, Trina, it's great to see you!" I exclaimed, sitting up straighter in my bed.

"I just found out that you're a patient here, Chris! What happened to you?" Trina replied with concern in her voice.

"Well, I'm not having any fun, that's for sure," I said, exasperated. "I'm sick. I had to have a biopsy of this bump on my neck. See?"

I gestured to the bandage on my neck. Trina leaned over to take a look.

"How long are you gonna be in the hospital?" she asked.

"I don't know," I replied, my tone whinier than I intended. "I have something called *Hodgkin's disease*. I'm gonna have another operation in a few days. They're taking out my spleen, whatever that is, and they have to biopsy some more lymph nodes. They say they'll know more after the surgery."

"What about school? Summer vacation is over in a few weeks," she reminded, but I needed no reminding.

"I don't know. I keep asking, but no one has an answer about that yet." I shrugged and dropped my hands in my lap. "It's boring sitting in this room all day. And hospital food is the worst."

"So, who says you have to sit?" Trina asked with a sparkle in her blue-green eyes. "Go put some clothes on, and we'll go for a walk to the cafeteria for some frozen yogurt."

Mouth wide open, I looked at her with disbelief and replied, "Daddy'll kill me if he sees me, or finds out I've gotten out of bed or left my room."

"No, he won't. But, if you're worried, we'll make sure he doesn't see you." Trina giggled.

It's no wonder that some of the nuns in our high school referred to Trina and me as *double trouble*.

"Okay," I said as I bounced out of bed, popped into the bathroom, changed into shorts and a tee shirt, and slipped on my docksiders. I ran a brush through my hair and washed my pale face. I looked terrible.

"Come on. Let's go."

Trina stuck her head out of my room and looked left then right, checking that the coast was clear. She gestured for me to follow her. We tiptoed down the hall to one of the stairways and quietly down three flights of steps to the main floor, through the lobby and up to the cafeteria, avoiding my dad's office. No one noticed us until we opened the cafeteria door and ran smack into my father's secretary, Cheryl. Her bright red hair fell in waves around her shoulders, and her readers hung on a beaded necklace and rested on the leopard print blouse straining over her ample chest.

"What are you doing out of bed, young lady?"

"Oh, umm, hi, Cheryl," I said, like it was the most natural thing in the world that I should be standing in front of her. I gave her my best smile. "Trina and I wanted to go for a walk and get some yogurt. It's boring in my room. Please don't tell my dad."

She paused, deciding what to do. She smiled at me.

"Make it quick and go straight back upstairs." Turning to Trina and half-heartedly scolding her, Cheryl said, "And you! What would your mom say about sneaking Christine out? You know better."

"It was an act of mercy. Chris's been eating hospital food for days," Trina volleyed back, blinking her innocent eyes.

Cheryl laughed.

"Christine, how would you like me to bring you a hero from the Oasis deli tomorrow for lunch? But you have to promise to stay in your room."

"That'd be totally awesome. I'll stay put."

Trina and I got our yogurts, topped them with strawberries and granola, and casually returned to my room the way we came. We ate and talked about starting school again. We wondered what our classes and teachers would be like—other than math. We already knew what that would be like since we'd have the same math teacher we had in ninth grade: the terrifying Sister Marie. I'd spent most of the year in *math detention*, staying after school every few days to correct quizzes where I got less than an eighty percent—which was often. Algebra and I didn't get along.

"I gotta go and meet my mom," Trina finally said with a sigh. "But now that I know you're here, I'll be back tomorrow, and maybe we could sit outside."

"Trina, are you kidding me?" I exclaimed, shocked at a suggestion even more outrageous than our yogurt jaunt.

"Fresh air is good for you," she said, grinning with mischief in her eyes.

My father walked in.

"Mr. Shields, hi. I'm going to meet my mom. Have a good night." Trina scurried out the door.

"Bye, Trina," my dad said, looking quizzically at the blur of a girl breezing past him through the doorway. Then he faced me. "I brought you a magazine."

"Wow, Daddy, thanks," I exclaimed looking at the cover and smiling at him. "I love the *Seventeen* Back to School issue, but I don't think I'm going back to school, though."

"We'll figure school out," my dad said. "Don't worry about that. Hey, listen, Cheryl told me that she'd like to bring you lunch tomorrow. What do you want from Oasis?"

"Oh my gosh! I'd love peppers and eggs," I replied, like this was the first I'd heard of it. "That's so awesome of her."

Daddy and I chatted for a few more minutes before he headed home. As he walked out the door, he called over his shoulder, "And, no more trips to the cafeteria, okay?"

Rolling my eyes at him, I sighed, "Oh, okay."

He didn't say anything about going outside.

On Thursday morning, I packed my overnight bag for the swim meet and headed to Florham Park, NJ for my ultrasound. After it was over, I met with Karen, Dr. Diehl's nurse, the radiologist, and another surgeon in the practice, as Dr. Diehl was in surgery. We chatted about the ultrasound, which was inconclusive.

The doctors suggested an MRI-guided biopsy if I wanted to consider breast conservation. I threw up my hands at everyone crammed in the tiny office and in my the- negotiations-have-ended voice announced, "No. No more tests. No more biopsies. I'm having a bilateral mastectomy. That's it."

One of the doctors tried to talk me out of it.

I looked at him with my eyebrows raised—Mom taught me well—and said, "I've made my decision."

Karen interjected, "We completely understand. You can speak to Dr. Diehl about it further. I can schedule an appointment with him for you."

"That would be great," I replied, my voice softening.

The doctors left the office, and turning to her computer to make the appointment, Karen said, "Your pathology report came in. I'll print it out. Be back in a minute."

She returned with the report and showed it to me, highlighting that I was estrogen and progesterone receptor positive, but HER2 negative. This meant I'd have surgery and no chemotherapy. I was relieved. I'd schedule the surgery quickly and get my life back to normal. Check.

As soon as I got in my car, I called Tim, my hands shaking. He picked up, as always, on my first ring.

"Hey sweetie. I got the pathology results," I said to my husband, the words spilling from my mouth. "I don't need chemo, only surgery—the result I was praying for. Thank God."

"That's the best news I've heard all week. Should we tell the kids now?" Tim asked.

"I don't want to do that to Tom before this meet. Let's stick with the plan and tell them all on Sunday while Katie's home."

"Sounds good," he said.

*Seemed like a good plan at the time.*

⌐⌐

## The Practical Reality

### Trust Yourself

One thing that survivors often say to me is that they wished they'd trusted themselves more, especially when they felt something was off or they were uncertain. Too often, it was easy for me to brush aside those feelings of disquietude or talk myself out of asking questions because:

*What do I know?*

*I'm being silly.*

*I'm overreacting.*

*I don't want to bother anyone.*

*I'm afraid.*

*They know what's best.*

When I think of all of the times I've done this and not listened to my inner voice, I've regretted it.

Trust yourself.

Trust your body.

Trust your mind.

If something feels off, don't stew on it or ignore it. Talk to your health care team. That being said, in the end, I recognized that I did the best I could do at the time with the information I had.

# Chapter 6
## How Not to Tell Your Kids You Have Cancer

To Do (3/11 to 3/13)
Take Tom to meet
Get pathology report again
Lunch w/Athena
Tell kids

TOM AND I WERE up early for the Lancaster, PA meet on Friday morning. I dropped Tom off for warm-ups and hung out in the car, drinking a mediocre cup of coffee from the hotel where we were staying.

When the time was right, I walked into the college athletic center where the meet was held. I joined the line of bleary-eyed parents and eventually made my way to the hot and muggy pool gallery. A couple of parents from Tom's team saw me as I walked in and waved. I joined our row and made small talk until the meet started. I watched my son swim his first event, the 100 yard backstroke, and have a solid swim.

After Tom showered and dressed, he met me outside the locker room. We drove back to the hotel and chatted about his swim. I noticed the tightness in my shoulders that I'd felt all week was gone.

"I'm going to take a nap, then get lunch with Joe and Ross," he said to me, perhaps sensing my newfound calm.

"That's fine, sweetie. I'm meeting Athena for lunch."

While I was driving to the restaurant to meet my friend, Katie called.

"Hi sweetie, are you on the road yet? Is everything okay?" I asked.

"I'm outside Albany. I've decided to break up with my boyfriend this weekend."

"Oh honey, I'm sorry. It wasn't working with him still being in high school?"

"Yeah, and he's completely focused on getting into college, so it was the combination of the stress and the distance. I think it's best to end it," Katie replied, her voice trailing off.

"I'm still sorry, though."

"It's okay, Mom, and thanks. I'm looking forward to a New Jersey bagel," Katie laughed. "But Mom, have you gotten the pathology report back yet?"

Even though I'd promised her that I'd tell her the results as soon as I had them, I didn't want to tell Katie I had breast cancer while she was driving on the New York State Thruway for hours alone.

"No, I'm still waiting to hear from the doctors. I'm not sure why this is taking so long. I'm in Lancaster now with Tom, and he had a nice swim this morning. I'll be home on Sunday after the meet is over. I'll see you then for lunch."

Ignoring my attempt to steer the conversation away from the pathology report, Katie replied, "That's strange, Mom. Weren't you expecting the report by now?"

"Well, um, Dr. Diehl said a week or so," I replied, pausing for a moment, and blurted, "I'm sure I'll hear soon."

"Okay, Mom. Tell Tom, 'Good luck and swim fast.' Bye."

I could tell from her voice she didn't believe me.

⤙⤚

My parents hid things from my siblings and me from the time we were kids until we were well into our twenties. When my grandma was diagnosed with breast cancer, I must have been in college or law school, and my mother didn't tell me about her mother's diagnosis. I only found out years later at a wedding when a relative happened to mention it to me.

"Oh, didn't you know that Grandma had breast cancer three years ago?"

*I didn't know because you folks, you collective brain trust of wisdom and experience, never told me.*

"No. No, I didn't. She's okay now, right?" I asked, trying to hide my annoyance at this continuous game.

"Yes, she's fine."

I confronted Mom afterwards. "Jeez, Mom. I didn't know Grandma had breast cancer. Why didn't you tell me when it was happening? This was important information not only for me, but for all of the women in the family."

The answer always was the same.

"I didn't want to worry you, and Grandma didn't want to tell anyone. She didn't want to upset the family."

"Come on," I replied, my frustration rising. "We're not kids any more. You don't have to protect us. It was important for us to know."

"Well, you know it now," my mom replied, purposely ignoring my exasperation.

"That's not the point," I sighed.

There was no sense in arguing—Mom wasn't going to change.

⤙⤚

When Tim and I married, and we talked about what we wanted for our family, we put honesty on the top of our list. I didn't want us to play the head games with our kids that my parents had played with my siblings and me.

But, in my moment of crisis, was I honest with my daughter?

Nope. I wasn't, even though I had a good reason for not telling her about my diagnosis right away. I was trying to protect her while she was driving home alone, and even though I intended to fill her and her brothers in after Tom's meet, my lie galled me.

I thought I was different from my parents.

*Perhaps not so much after all.*

⌒

Athena was already at the brew pub next to the pool when I got there. When I walked up to our lunch table, she stood and gave me a big hug.

"I'm so happy for you. No chemo. That's great."

I had told Athena my news in a call earlier that morning.

"I can't tell you how relieved I am," I responded. "It'll be easier to tell the kids on Sunday. I'll schedule the surgery as soon as I can. I have to find a plastic surgeon."

"Do you want me to ask around for you?"

"Sure, ask away," I replied, grateful for her help.

We turned the conversation back to the swim meet and our kids' swims. I felt calmer knowing that there was the beginning of a plan to get past this breast cancer diagnosis and back to my life.

Early the next morning, before Tom woke up for the remainder of the swim meet, I sat in the dim hotel living room with my computer, checking my email and the news, when my cell phone rang. Dr. Diehl's number appeared on my caller ID. A sense of cold moved into my chest and stomach.

"Good morning, Chris," Dr. Diehl said. "I have news about your HER2 marker."

"Hi, Dr. Diehl. Karen told me on Thursday about my HER2 marker. It's negative."

Dr. Diehl paused. Then, in his most his authoritative and precise doctor voice, he said, "No. No, it's not."

He didn't say this unkindly, but it felt as if he had sucker punched me in the gut. I tried to breathe, but the air couldn't find its way into my lungs.

"The HER2 results Karen shared with you were, in my view, inconclusive," he continued. "I ordered a more precise test that shows you're HER2 positive. This is the most important piece of information, Chris, so I had to make sure. You'll need neoadjuvant chemotherapy after all—that is, before surgery. I know this isn't what you wanted to hear. I'm sorry."

"Oh," I whispered and leaned further into the sofa where Tom and I had laughed together the night before.

"I hate to keep giving you bad news. I'm afraid you'll stop taking my calls," Dr. Diehl said in an attempt to make me laugh. "I'll send the reports to your oncologist. You need to see him as soon as possible."

"Oh, don't worry. I'll always take your calls," I whispered, ending the call.

My cell phone slipped from my hand and onto the sofa cushion. I rested my head on my knees trying to process this new development.

The phone rang again a few minutes later.

"Hi, honey, why are you calling this early?' I asked, hoping Tim wouldn't notice the shakiness in my voice.

"Hi sweetheart. I need to tell you something." Tim's voice sounded strained as he blurted, "Katie cornered me last night and asked what was going on with you. I couldn't lie to her. I had to tell her."

*Of course he did. The Corrigan side of our family cannot keep anything in the vault.*

"Christ, Tim. What did you tell her?" I replied, my voice rising as I stood up and began pacing the small hotel living area, my heart beating rapidly again.

"I told her you had breast cancer and needed surgery. She's really upset."

"Well, I hung up with Dr. Diehl a few minutes ago," I said, pausing for emphasis, "and it turns out I need chemo, too. This is exactly why I wanted to wait. Jesus, Tim," I chastised. I knew I was taking Dr. Diehl's news out on him, but I couldn't stop.

"I'm sorry," Tim sighed. "Here, Katie wants to talk to you."

"Mom, what the fuck," Katie sobbed into the phone. "You lied to me. You promised me you'd tell me what was going on, and you didn't."

My heart splintered, hearing her cry, my Scorpio child, with her stinger-sharp voice and heart on her sleeve.

What could I say? Katie *was* right: I had kept information from her. Sure, I had a good reason, but still.

The plan I had in my mind for the five of us to gather at the kitchen table, share the news and a collective moment of grief, like a Norman Rockwell tableau, lay shattered at my feet. My need to control the flow of information to ease the kids' pain and the fear hadn't helped at all, just like my parents' silence and expectations didn't help me when I was a teen.

I had broken the promise I made to Katie weeks earlier, and to myself years earlier.

*There'll be no change until I change. I have to accept that I can't control this.*

"You're right, Katie," I sighed in defeat. "I did, and I'm terribly sorry. I wanted to tell you and the boys at the same time. And, as luck would have it, what Daddy told you is wrong."

"What? What do you mean?"

"I just spoke with Dr. Diehl. He ordered another pathology test, apparently a more accurate one. It turns out I need chemo *and* surgery."

"I'm going to go back to Vermont today instead of Sunday," she said slowly and quietly.

I started crying.

*What we sow, we reap.*

"Katie, I'm sorry. I didn't mean to hurt you sweet girl, and I didn't want to tell you this way. I hope you can forgive me."

I sniffed, brushed the tears from my face, cognizant of how badly I messed this up and continued, "Please be careful driving to Vermont and text me when you're back. I love you, Katie."

The words hung between us.

"Love you too, Mom," she said softly before she ended the call.

*A measure of absolution.*

⌒

Katie had every right to be angry. Her anger then, like mine a year later, burned like a flash of searing lightning. Both of us felt like we could have split a tree or torn apart an entire kitchen. And that's just how I felt when I learned that my parents never told me about the type of tumor I had when I had Hodgkin's.

On a May morning, a light spring breeze rustling through my kitchen as I sat at my desk in the quiet house working on an assignment for my writing class. The boys were at school, Katie at college, and Tim at work. Ollie, my devoted Cavalier King Charles spaniel, lay on the floor next to my feet snoozing. I could hear the catbirds calling and chipmunks chittering in the garden outside the kitchen door.

It was almost noon, and I needed a stretch. I decided to get the mail from the box at the end of our driveway. I walked by my garden beds filled with late blooms—lingering daffodils and lilacs, so much of spring's promise. I pulled the mail and saw an envelope from Memorial Sloan Kettering. I knew what was inside: After hearing my writing teacher lecture on the importance of being *journalistic* in our stories and seeking out factual support where we could, I had decided to request my old medical records to find out more about my Hodgkin's experience in 1981. The information might well fill in the gaps in my hazy memories.

I returned to my desk, tore open the envelope, and started reading my hospital records. I flipped through pages of old lab results until I found my Outpatient Progress Record that listed all of my radiation treatments. I confirmed my memory about the dates of treatment and how much of high school I missed. As I continued to scan the progress record, I read, "During this time, she tolerated her treatments well and she had a good response to the mediastinal mass."

I stopped reading. I had no idea what those words meant. I don't remember my parents or Dr. Forte ever telling me that I had a *mediastinal mass*. I would have remembered that.

I turned to my computer and immediately searched on Google to uncover the term's meaning. Imagine my surprise when I learned thirty-six years later that I didn't have a tumor in my neck, ever. Rather, the lymph nodes in my neck were enlarged because I had a fucking tumor in the middle of my chest.

I bolted upright, sending my desk chair flying back, and swore out loud, "Goddammit, Mom and Dad. If you both weren't freakin' dead, I'd kill you! I cannot believe this shit continues even today! What the hell else didn't you tell us?"

I slammed the stack of records on my desk. I wanted to throw something across the room; I wanted to punch a wall. Instead, I stormed over to the dishwasher.

I smacked the dishwasher door down. The glasses and plates rattled inside the racks.

I opened our kitchen cutlery drawer, threw in the knives and forks, and slammed it closed. Bam!

"I hope you're listening up there you two, because I. Am. Royally. Pissed!" I ranted, borrowing a favorite phrase from my mom's arsenal and raising my fists toward the ceiling. "Did you get that? Pissed!!" I shouted.

I grabbed pots from the dishwasher and hurled them into the drawers. Crash!

I slammed a frying pan onto the stove.

"Really, who does this? Who does this to their kids? What the hell was wrong with you two?" I yelled as I kicked the pot drawer closed and rattled its contents.

The dog scurried from his spot in the middle of the floor and cowered in the farthest corner beneath my desk.

I stood in the middle of the kitchen panting. I looked at my fitness watch: my pulse was in the cardio range.

*Jesus.* I needed to calm down.

I collapsed on a stool at the counter and took a long swig from my water bottle. I crossed my arms on the counter and rested my head on them. In a moment of painful clarity, I knew why breast cancer is one of the most common secondary cancers in female Hodgkin's survivors. I knew why my grandma made me promise to wear a Sacred Heart of Jesus scapula over my chest while I was in treatment. I knew why Dr. Forte told me at age twenty-one to start my mammograms in my thirties. All the radiation I received was aimed right at my chest—at the tumor that everyone knew about, everyone except me.

Thanks to my parents' need to *protect* me, I've always told any doctor who was taking a medical history that I had Stage IIA Hodgkin's with the primary tumor site in my neck, which was wrong—wrong by a lot. I guess this is why, when I first told my current oncologist about my Hodgkin's and that the original tumor was in my neck, his face clouded over as if he were trying to process something that didn't make sense. While I noticed his reaction at the time and found it puzzling, I didn't ask him about it, so secure was I in my narrative.

I could understand that my parents probably didn't want to add to an already traumatic experience when I was fourteen, but this information was important for me to know as an adult because of all the risks radiation would pose to my future health.

Why didn't they come clean when I was older? Perhaps they thought they were protecting me somehow, like I wanted to protect my own kids. Perhaps they had faith that advances in medicine would allow me to handle whatever the Fates sent my way later in life. Or, perhaps, they simply wanted to forget.

*At this point, does it matter? Probably not. At this point, can I let it go? Yes. But I don't think I'll completely escape my history.*

⌒

After the calls from Dr. Diehl, Tim, and Katie, I sat in the hotel room in silence, trying to make sense of it all.

I was pissed because I lied to Katie.

I was pissed because Tim didn't.

I was pissed because my doctor's call had shredded my perfect plan of putting breast cancer behind me quickly and getting back to normal life as soon as possible.

I needed to clear my head, so I took a shower before waking Tom and facing another day of swimming and small talk. I stood under the water-conserving showerhead and let the tepid water trickle over me.

Clarity wouldn't come. Instead, my mind turned back to those old, terrible memories—the ones I never wanted to think about from early September 1981, when I began radiation therapy at Memorial Sloan Kettering in New York.

⌒

I opened the hospital doors on York Avenue when a sickly-sweet odor enveloped me and turned my stomach (that day, and every other day). As my parents and I found our way to the outpatient radiology department, the smell stayed with us—on our clothes, in our noses, on our skin.

We passed so many sick people, including young children, who were lying on stretchers in the hallways or sitting in wheelchairs outside of their rooms. Many of them were attached to IV poles with bags of different colored fluids and long tubes winding their way to the needles secured to their arms with tape or snaked beneath their hospital gowns. Some of the kids had lost their hair; some wore knitted caps to hide their baldness. The color had drained from their faces, which were thin and gaunt. There was no light in their eyes.

"Mom, what's wrong with them? What's in the IVs?" I whispered to her, my voice trembling as we passed them one by one in the hallways.

Mom gave me one of her looks that signaled it was neither the time nor place for such questions. I ignored her.

"They look really sick, Mom," I said, my voice rising with worry.

She raised her eyebrows, another signal that I was treading too close to the line.

"They are sick, Chrissy," she whispered through barely parted lips. "Very, very sick."

"That won't happen to me, will it?" I asked, horrified at the thought of going bald or being stuck in this terrible place.

"No. No. That will not happen to you," Mom said, with far more emphasis and volume than she meant.

Despite my mom's assurance, the sight of these young patients still scared me. I didn't understand what was wrong with them or why I had to go to this special place for treatment when I just had Hodgkin's disease.

I wasn't as sick as these kids. I didn't look like them or even feel sick.

I couldn't bear to look at them, so day after day I stared at the beige linoleum floor as we walked by them.

⤙

As quickly as I had brought them out, I shoved those memories back into the Box.

*Chemotherapy couldn't be the answer to my breast cancer. It simply couldn't.*

I turned off the shower, got dressed, and woke Tom. I had to get out of the hotel room.

As we drove to our favorite diner in Lancaster, the one where all the swimmers go, I replayed all of the morning's conversations in my head, trying to come up with a plan. There had to be a way to get out of chemo.

Once we were seated, the waitress appeared with a coffee pot in hand and took our orders. Tom and I chatted about his race later that morning as he attacked his French toast with gusto. I picked at my spinach omelet that tasted like dust.

After we made our way to the pool, Tom headed to the locker room while I meandered to the spectator gallery and scanned for an empty spot to sit. My friend, Diane, caught my eye and waved, gesturing that I should come up and join her. Her son, Joe, was one of Tom's closest friends.

I climbed the stairs to where Diane was sitting, and she moved over to make a place for me. I collapsed onto the bench next to her.

"Hey, Diane, thanks for the seat," I gasped.

"Chris, are you okay?" Diane asked, her voice filled with concern.

I shook my head and slowly whispered, "I was diagnosed with breast cancer about a week ago, and I found out this morning that I need to have chemo."

Diane put her arm around my shoulder and gave me a gentle squeeze.

"Oh, Chris, I'm sorry. You must be overwhelmed. And to learn it at a swim meet."

"I know. Ridiculous, right? You can't make this shit up."

"Did you know my husband had cancer?" Diane asked.

"No, I had no idea. Is he okay now?" I replied.

"Yes, he's fine. He had a rare melanoma a few years ago. So, I get what you must be going through," she sympathized. "Did you tell the kids yet?"

"Not the boys. Katie knows. Tim told her last night, and I spoke with her this morning. She didn't take it well." I sighed and continued, "I didn't want to tell Tom before the meet, so Tim and I will tell the boys tomorrow night when we get home."

"That makes sense," Diane replied, shaking her head in agreement. "You can call me anytime you need, you know that, right? And tell Tom he can call Joe any time; he gets it."

I smiled at Diane, heartened to know Tom had a friend in Joe and his family when he might need them.

"Yes, I do, and I will."

The next morning, Tom and I left Lancaster after his last race, both of us tired and glad to be headed home. For the two-hour drive back to New Jersey, Tom slept blissfully, oblivious to the swirling mess in my head.

After dinner later that night, Tim and I remained at the kitchen table with the boys. I pushed my shoulders back and dug down to my core, to that place where I imagined a silver flame burned—the essence of my best and strongest self—and said, "Tom, James, we have to tell you something important."

The boys looked at me, then Tim.

"I have breast cancer." I continued quickly, "My doctors caught it early, but I need chemotherapy and surgery."

"Are you going to lose your hair?" Tom asked, his eyes wide with horror.

"Probably, but I'll get a wig or wear a baseball cap."

James started to cry. "Mom, are you going to die?" He got up from his chair, wrapped his arms around my neck, and rested his head on my shoulder.

"Pray, God, not from this," I answered as I stroked James' blond head. "Listen to me, both of you. This isn't going to be easy. Sometimes, bad things happen. People get sick. We don't know why. We're all going to get through this together."

"Mom has great doctors, boys, and they are going to take good care of her. So, please don't worry," Tim added.

"You, and Katie, and Daddy are the most important things in the world to me," I said, my voice breaking. "You are both going to go to school, swim, go to Scouts, run, and do all the things you always do. I will do my very best to keep your lives as normal as possible."

The boys nodded. I kissed James on his forehead and wiped his tears away. I stood and asked them to help clear the table while Tom took the trash out to the garage.

Several minutes went by. I opened the back door and found Tom standing in the dark.

"Hey sweetie, are you okay? Come inside."

"Yeah, I'm fine," he said, his voice thick.

Tom brushed by me as he walked in the house and avoided looking at me.

⸻

More than a year later, Tom told me after hearing the news, he had cried in the dark, as I thought he had.

He cried because he didn't want me to be sick.

He cried because he didn't want his life to change.

He cried because he knew it would.

⸻

If I could travel back in time to that evening, I would have placed my hands on my own shoulders and given myself a hard shake. What the hell was I thinking, telling the boys I'd try to keep our lives *normal?*

Nothing about having cancer is normal. My entire family and I knew that thirty-five years ago.

Was it normal for my parents to drive from Staten Island to Manhattan four days a week for my radiation therapy? Was it normal for me to throw up into a plastic basin as I lay in the back seat of the car on the way home after almost every treatment? What was normal about only going to high school one day a week and trying to catch up on the weekends with classmates' notes? What was normal about spending hour after hour alone in my bedroom listening to Stevie Nicks on my scratchy stereo, her voice my only company, while the rest of my family went to work or school, had dinner together, and worried?

It wasn't normal.
It was survival.
And it was the best my parents could do.
It would be the best I could do, too.

# Chapter 7
## Surrender

To Do (3/14)
Get out of chemo
Schedule surgery

ON MONDAY MORNING, I dressed for my appointment with my oncologist, Dr. Abbasi, like I was going to take a deposition:

Grey cashmere turtleneck, silver necklace and earrings, tailored black pants and black loafers—perfectly professional. Check

Nails, manicured pale pink. Check

Notebook with numbered questions and folders labeled *Biopsy* and *Pathology Reports*, organized in my tote. Check

Using my years of lawyering, I planned to argue my way out of chemo. As I drove to my oncologist's office in Morristown, I reviewed the facts as I understood them. I fashioned my arguments as to why those facts couldn't possibly mean I needed chemotherapy. I strode into Oncology & Hematology Specialists' office and checked in. As I waited, I looked around the beige box-like room. Other patients with pallid, resigned faces were waiting. Some wore knitted caps or turbans similar to those I remembered on the patients in Sloan Kettering's hallways.

I startled when I heard my name and followed one of the nurses into an office. A large, dark cherry desk filled the middle of the room. A tissue box sat on the desk's corner within easy reach of the two chairs facing it. I sat, then placed my folders and notebook on the desk. I pushed the tissues aside.

Sporting a navy suit and starched white shirt, with a stethoscope draped around his neck, Dr. Abbasi bounded into the room. I stood and extended my hand. Dr. Abbasi took it, pulling me into a gentle hug. My spine softened as I rested my head on his shoulder.

"How are you doing?" he asked.

"I've been better," I replied. The words stuck in my throat. "And you?"

"I'm blessed," he answered. His bright smile disarmed me.

Dr. Abbasi breezed around the desk, clapped his hands, and announced, "Are you ready? Because here we go!"

I raised my eyebrows. Where was I *going?* I had inconsistent pathology reports—one indicating that I needed chemotherapy and one suggesting otherwise. I wanted a different explanation, preferably one that didn't involve that word.

*I'm handing you what's been marked as Exhibits A and B.*

I sat as he studied the reports. I opened my notebook and ticked through my questions as if I were examining a witness. I looked up. With his hand across his dark moustache and finger resting on his cheek, Dr. Abbasi sat silently. His brown eyes radiated warmth and compassion.

I crossed my arms and returned his gaze. He stood, then walked over to sit beside me.

*I never had a witness do that before.*

*That's because he's not a witness, Christine.*

He put the reports on the desk and explained the differences between the two like professor to student.

"The second test showing that you are HER2 positive is far more accurate than the first that shows the negative result."

"Can't we do another test? Like a tie-breaker or something?" I countered.

"We can't ignore the positive test, Chris," he insisted, pointing to his notes. "Look at these numbers. Your cancer cell duplication rate is over twice the high average."

Dr. Abbasi returned to his chair and typed some notes on his computer. He ran his hand over his graying temples and turned toward me.

"You need six cycles of chemotherapy followed by another twelve cycles of anti-HER2 therapy. The first six cycles will take about four months, through mid-July. The anti-HER2 therapy will take eight more months. About a year of treatment."

I couldn't speak. My stomach heaved.

*A freakin' year of my life?*

He paused for a moment, sizing up my mood, and went on. "It wasn't like this ten years ago, you know. By the time of your surgery, God willing, the tumor will be melted away."

He leaned back in his chair and brought his hands together against his chest, fingertips touching, as if in prayer. He waited.

His words steeped. The minutes passed. I understood what he was telling me, what all the test results meant. Ten years ago with an aggressive cancer I wouldn't have had this treatment option—and in that moment I knew Dr. Abbasi had my back.

I wouldn't argue anymore. I couldn't argue anymore. I closed my eyes and prayed for strength. I placed my hands palms up in my lap, swallowed the lump in my throat and said, "Well, God doesn't give us more than we can bear."

"That's a verse in the Quran," Dr. Abbasi replied. "'Allah does not burden a soul beyond that it can bear.' I'm Muslim."

"I'm Catholic."

"I'm pretty sure it's in your scriptures, too."

I thought I'd quoted from my scriptures a moment ago. But, since I wasn't good at chapter and verse Bible recitation, I decided to check my New American Bible when I got home.

In St. Paul's first letter to the Corinthians, he wrote: *God is faithful and will not let you be tried beyond your strength; but with the trial he will also provide a way out, so that you may be able to bear it.* Those words made more sense than the sentiment I'd offered earlier. I could be tried to the limits of my strength. I would be tried. But, God in his mercy would provide a way out so that I could bear the trial. Whether through God's grace or good karma, Dr. Abbasi became my way out. I believe that Dr. Abbasi would say it was God's will. Whichever view, he allowed me to bear the months to come, though I didn't know that then.

After Dr. Abbasi and I established our faith traditions, I steered the conversation back to more pressing matters. I asked him the question I dreaded because I already knew the answer.

"Am I, am I going to lose my hair?" I faltered.

I liked my thick, wavy, brown hair. Being bald would remind me (and everyone else) of how sick I was. I also knew my hair wouldn't be the same when it grew back *(it isn't)*.

I'd lost a big amount of my hair when I had radiation therapy. In my mind's eye I still could see the clumps lodged in the shower drain, like a waterlogged rat at my feet.

I turned my head away and fixed my gaze out the window. I knew

Tom would be horrified. What teenage boy wanted a bald mom? And Tim, he would never say anything, but he'd hate my bald head too.

"Yes," Dr. Abbasi replied, nudging the box of tissues toward me. I took one and wiped my eyes.

I appreciated his candor. He didn't downplay or minimize this loss by reminding me that my hair would grow back. He didn't say it was *just hair* as so many others would point out.

"Here's my suggestion," Dr. Abbasi continued, "Get a wig now that matches your hair color and style. I'll give you a script."

"A script for a wig?" I asked, puzzled at the thought.

"No," he bantered, "a cranial prosthesis."

I laughed for the first time since Dr. Diehl called me with the news two days ago. I gathered my folders and notebook.

"One more thing," Dr. Abbasi added. "You need to schedule surgery to have a port catheter implanted."

"What's that?" I asked.

"It's a little device that's implanted under the skin with a tube that gets inserted into a vein in your chest," he explained. "The chemotherapy medications will be infused through it rather than an IV."

"Why can't we do this by IV? Why do I need surgery?" I demanded, annoyed that cancer required yet another thing, another procedure, another intrusion into my life.

"The medications are very strong and will damage the veins in your arms. It has to be done this way." Dr. Abbasi calmly replied. "Please call Dr. Diehl to get the procedure scheduled. I want you to start chemo next week. Here's my cell," he said as he scribbled his number on the back of his card and handed it to me. "You can call or text me anytime."

I walked toward the door, paused, and glanced over my shoulder.

"Thank you," I said.

Unlike my appointment with Dr. Abbasi, I don't remember much about my first meeting with Dr. Charles, my radiation oncologist at Sloan Kettering, other than his appearance. He was tall, thin, and gray-haired, with a stern demeanor.

I don't remember ever seeing Dr. Charles smile. Not that I would have noticed; he didn't speak to me. He addressed only my parents as if I wasn't in the room.

I didn't like him.

With hindsight, I think differently. Dr. Charles gave me back high school, the chance to go to college and law school, to have a career, to marry the love of my life, and to have my children. I never thanked him. I should have.

I wish I'd figured that out sooner.

⌒

## The Practical Reality
**DigniCap®**

Patients receiving chemotherapy for breast or other cancers say that one of the hardest things about treatment is hair loss. It was for me. With hair loss comes the understanding that they are really sick, which not only can impact their mental and emotional health, but also that of their partners, children, and family. It can be quite disconcerting, or even frightening, for family members to see a person whom they have known to look a certain way, without hair and looking unwell.

Thanks to advances in technology, there is a scalp cooling system designed to reduce chemotherapy-induced hair loss in certain (not all) types of cancer, called DigniCap®. By cooling the scalp, the blood flow to the scalp area is reduced so that less chemotherapy reaches the hair cells. Hair cells that are not exposed to the full dose of chemotherapy may be able to survive. If you're worried about hair loss, speak to your doctors about whether this technology is available to you. If so, contact your insurance company to determine whether the use of this device is covered.

**Dental Care**

Chemotherapy messes with your dental hygiene, along with everything else. Because chemotherapy weakens the immune system and because the mouth is full of nasty bacteria, you probably can't have your teeth cleaned or have other dental procedures while you're having chemotherapy, if your doctors are anything like mine. So get your teeth cleaned and any needed dental work before you start.

# Part Two

## THE ONLY WAY OUT

# Chapter 8
## Do the Thing You Think You Cannot Do

To Do (3/24)
Boys' schedules
Backpack
Learn about side effects
Decline chemo turban

THE ALARM BLARED AT 5:30 in the morning on my first day of chemo. I nestled back under Tim's arm, drawing strength from him. We'd made love the night before, taking comfort in each other's familiar bodies. After a few minutes, I slipped out from under his arm, stood, and stretched. Tim rolled into my spot as he always did. "Spot thief," I whispered to him, as I padded across our soft gray chenille carpet toward the bathroom.

I'd splurged on the carpet a few years earlier, notwithstanding Tim's initial protests about its cost. But, I wouldn't give that rug back.

We both hate having cold feet. And I couldn't get cold feet about what I would face that day. The first step to the end would begin today. Once I set myself on this path, there would be no return. With each treatment, I would be one step closer to my mastectomy day.

In the shower I let the water, warmer than I liked, rain over me. I needed its heat to melt the icy fear in my core. Breathing in the scent from my favorite soap, I prayed for courage to face the day.

I stepped out of the shower and wrapped a fluffy white towel around me. I stood in front of the mirror and wiped the steam away. I pulled the towel off and rubbed it over my head. I spritzed my hair with styling gel then combed it with my fingers, feeling its thickness under my palms. I stared at my image and willed myself to remember what I looked like, with the wave of my hair running left to right.

I slathered moisturizer over my smooth skin, avoiding the quarter-sized protrusion under my right collarbone where the port was, the skin still tender from the surgery three days earlier.

My middle-aged breasts and tummy were soft and round. I traced my finger around my areolas and grazed my nail over my nipples, now erect. I felt their warmth. I traced my finger along the long scar running from the blue-black dot tattoo beneath my breastbone to the little blue-black dot tattoo above my pubic bone, my Hodgkin's stigmata. Over the years, the tattoos—each about the size of a pen tip—had faded on the edges, but their centers remained dark, immutable like my memories of that time.

I rested my hands on my hips and looked down at the untamed tuft of gray-black curls.

I willed myself to remember what my body felt like under my hands.

Before it started.

While I was still whole, and my body was still my own.

*Yes, I see you standing there, looking so smug. You've been waiting thirty-five years for this day. I hope you're ready for the cocktail that's coming your way. It will destroy you.*

The Beast said nothing.

*You listen to me, and you listen well. You can take my hair. You can take my breasts. You will not take me. I beat you once. I'll do it again or die trying.*

The Beast stepped back, then skulked away.

~

Pushing those thoughts aside, I went to get dressed. I pulled on my favorite running tights and a cozy sweater. I would be sitting on my ass all day attached to an IV infusion pump so I might as well be comfortable.

I crept downstairs to the kitchen and made coffee. I sat at my desk like I did every morning, checking my email and making sure that the boys' schedules were laid out for Tim. I had to be at Dr. Abbasi's office by 7:15 a.m. to have blood tests, meet with one of the physician assistants to review the treatment's possible side effects, then start my first cycle. I checked my backpack—iPad, charger, book, water bottle, yogurt, banana. Tim would take the boys to school and meet me at Dr. Abbasi's later.

I heard the ping of a text: Katie's.

*Good luck today, Mom.*

Upon my arrival at Dr. Abbasi's, the receptionist handed me a small gift bag. I looked at her, bewildered. She explained the bag contained anti-nausea medications— one for before chemo, one for after—and a bottle of another medication to take home as Jen, my sister, texted me.

*Thinking of you! Be strong.*

While I waited to be called for my labs, I looked at an older gentleman sitting in a chair opposite me. He looked familiar—maybe a swim official I'd seen at meets over the years? If he was the official I was remembering, he looked much thinner than he did the last time I saw him at a meet. I didn't want to stare so I looked at my phone.

After my labs, Tim arrived, and we met with the physician assistant to learn about the fun I would have over the next four months. She told me I might become constipated from the anti-nausea medication, so I'd need a laxative—although after a few days I would probably have diarrhea. My sense of taste would change. My mouth and throat would get dry and sore. I could get a rash on my hands and feet. My eyes might tear constantly. I would get more and more fatigued as treatment progressed, because side effects were cumulative. The list went on and on.

As I listened to the parade of horrors and signed the form saying I understood it all, part of me couldn't imagine that any or all of it would happen. Side effects were statistical, right? What were the odds I'd experience all of them?

*Pretty good, apparently.*

I followed the physician assistant to the infusion room as Tim trailed behind us. The room was a large rectangle with a dozen dark-purple reclining chairs, each with an IV pole and infusion pump, lining the room's perimeter on three sides, with the nurse's station and blanket warmers along the fourth. The room was bright from the institutional lighting and two sets of windows. Two flat screen TVs played CNN and the *Today* show.

I found a chair next to a window and dropped my backpack onto the floor. Tim pulled up a folding chair, his jaw clenched in stress. I imagined he was remembering his dad, seeing the life leave him over months of treatment for metastatic prostate cancer.

"Hey, if this is too much to handle, I'll be fine. You can go. It's okay."

"I'll stay for a little while," replied Tim, squeezing my hand.

One of the nurses came over to my chair to attach the IV to my port. She asked me if I wanted her to spray a topical anesthetic on my skin before she stabbed me with the IV.

"No," I replied, rolling my eyes. "I want to feel *all* the pain."

She stood with her mouth open, not quite sure what to do.

"I'm kidding. I'm kidding," I laughed. "Spray away."

"I want you to breathe in and hold it, okay?"

I nodded, inhaled and looked away.

"One, two, three, done," she said in a crisp tone

I released my breath.

"Did it hurt?" Tim asked, his brow furrowed.

"No worse than any other needle stick. I bet it'd be worse without the spray, though. It made my skin super cold." I hoped my words would ease some of Tim's worry.

Another nurse came over with the first bags of medications. She asked me my date of birth and after I gave the correct answer, started the infusion party. She also told me I'd receive Benadryl and a steroid to prevent any allergic reactions. Good news. These would knock me out for a few hours. Then I took my anti-nausea pills and read my book, *Brooklyn* by Colm Tóibín.

Tim and I didn't say much. The only way out was through one drip, one bag, one hour, one day at a time. We would do this because we had no choice. As Dr. Abbasi told me the week before, "It has to be done this way." When we no longer had choices, what was left but forbearance?

When I was in treatment for Hodgkin's, my mom often reminded me, "This, too, will pass." She was right. This would too.

After about an hour, Tim looked up from his iPad, then said, "I'm going to work for a few hours. My office is sending dinner tonight."

My heart sunk. Tim would have stayed if I'd asked. But I knew he had to go.

I smiled and said, "I'll text you when I am finished. It's gonna be a long day."

Tim kissed me goodbye, turned and walked quickly down the hallway to the exit. As I watched him go, my bravado faded. I wanted to run after him and beg, "Please don't leave me with all these sick people. I'm scared."

Even though I didn't want to face the infusion room alone, I wouldn't do that to him. To stay all day was going to be too hard for him. I knew he needed the refuge of his office, of staying busy, to keep his own fears and memories at bay.

*Come on, Christine. You can do this. You're stronger than you know.*

I didn't feel strong. Not at all.

I glanced around the room. A young man wearing a knit ski cap was rapidly typing on his laptop. A tall, gaunt, woman was asleep under a blanket. She had on a pink-beribboned baseball cap and bright pink lipstick. I made a mental note not to forget to put on my lipstick. Wearing a good lipstick color flipped the bird at the Beast. I liked that.

The man I thought was a swim official was sleeping in a chair a few feet from me. At his feet, I saw a little drawstring bag with *Arena*, a brand of racing swimsuit printed on it.

What were the odds that that the man across from me was Jack, whom I'd watched officiate hundreds of meets over the years, and who even had told Katie and Tom that they'd been disqualified at one time or another?

*Pretty good, apparently.*

A short while later my phone lit up. Tom was checking to see how I was doing. Tim's brothers and my friends texted and offered words of support and encouragement. One friend sent me a couple of jokes and started what would become a tri-weekly comedy-fest. Their care and attention heartened me during this long first day.

⌒

A day or two earlier, I had received a note from Peg, Tim's aunt and inveterate letter writer. Peg had short brown hair, dancing eyes, and a hearty laugh. I met Peg when Tim and I were dating in college and she was undergoing chemotherapy for lymphoma.

In her note, Peg reminded me that she was forty-nine when she was in treatment, the same age I was. Peg wrote, "It's so shocking in the beginning to hear that awful diagnosis. And you get through it by putting one foot in front of the other. But all the time you'll truly be carried along by the enormous strength that emanates from those who love you. None of us ever goes through this alone."

When I first read Peg's words, I had dismissed them. I viewed the treatment as my test of strength. I would get through it by sheer force of will.

Yet, on that first long day, I came to understand what Peg meant. I was humbled by the realization and grateful for it.

⌣

Late in the morning, volunteers from the American Cancer Society arrived pushing carts—one loaded with fruit, juice, and bagels, and the other with turbans, baseball caps, pillows, and throws.

*Is this what happens? You get cancer then become a cancer volunteer?*

One of the volunteers must have noticed that I was a new arrival. She sat down next to me and asked if she could tell me about the various support services for cancer patients.

I nodded. She went right into her spiel, leaving me with a stack of booklets and a plastic accordion folder to put them all in. Another volunteer quickly took her place and offered me juice and a bagel. The last gray-haired volunteer to stop by my chair was, as I would come to think of her, *the turban lady.*

"Hello, dear. Is this your first day of treatment?"

"Yes."

"Do you mind my asking what type of cancer you have?"

"Breast."

"Do you want one of these?" she offered, waving a pink velour turban in front of me. "You know, for when your hair falls out," she added.

"No, thank you."

"Are you sure?"

"Yes. Very."

"We have other colors," she insisted.

"I don't care for them," I sighed, hoping she'd get the hint.

"They keep your head warm, too."

"I'm good. Thanks."

⌒

When I lost my hair a few weeks later, I started wearing Buffs, headwear for outdoor activities like hiking or rock climbing. They came in bright, fun patterns, and I wore them like big head bands. The turban lady did not like my Buff. Without fail on every treatment day she'd stop by my chair, stare at my Buff and offer me another turban.

"Look, this one has a flower. Do you want it?" she asked, with her head cocked and eyes ever hopeful that this was the day I'd see the beauty in velour.

*Not if that was the last thing that I had to wear while naked and stranded on the North Pole.*

"No, thank you."

⌒

Thinking back to those early exchanges, I ask myself why I had been such a bitch about those hats. The volunteer was trying to be helpful. I could have humored her, taken one, and ditched it on the way out of the office. But that didn't occur to me, because the chemo turban announced to the world, "I'm bald and have cancer, because there is no other reason to wear such a thing." I hated the idea that other people would see me in one of them and do any of the following:

Give me the pity stare.

Engage me in conversation about what was wrong.

Proceed to tell me about every other friend, relative, and neighbor they knew who had cancer and whether they lived or died.

Suggest that I consider the latest Internet cancer *cure*.

No. I would meet the Beast on my terms, wearing a sporty headband, not one of those stupid hats or the wig that I quickly came to hate.

Did that stop people from giving me the sympathy stare at ShopRite? Probably not, but it let me walk with my head held up. I was still myself on the inside—that was good enough.

⌐

The first day limped along, and after receiving a dose of Benadryl, I slipped into that hazy space between sleep and wake. As the television's chatter and the buzz in the room grew distant, images from my first day at Memorial Sloan Kettering rose out of the Box. As much as I didn't want to think about them, I couldn't stop these images from replaying in my head . . .

⌐

I saw myself topless, on a cold, hard table in a darkened room, with a red laser light grid beamed across my chest. A person in the shadows—man, woman, nurse, doctor; I couldn't tell—was holding a needle used to tattoo twelve dots across my chest, abdomen and back, as a guide for directing the beams of radiation.

"It hurts. I want it to stop, please," I begged my mom. She was standing next to me, holding my hand.

"It's only a few more. They're no worse than shots," my mom said in her matter-of-fact nurse's voice.

"Yes, they are," I cried, squeezing her hand as hard as I could. "They burn."

My mom tried a little humor. "Imagine your friends' faces when you tell them you have twelve tattoos," she joked.

"Oh my gosh, Mom," I said and pulled back my hand. "I'm never telling anyone." I balled my hands into two fists at my side.

The person doing the tattooing reminded me to stay still, which was hard to do since I was crying and freezing.

"We're almost done; just hang on for a few more minutes," the tattoo artist said.

"Stop! It hurts!"

"We can't. Then we'd have to set up the guides again," the person replied. "And it would delay the next appointment."

"Come on, Chris, you need to be brave," my mom added.

"I'm trying, but I don't want to be here. I don't want to do this."

After a few more needle sticks, the tattooing was over. The burning pain subsided, and I stopped crying.

I pulled the thin cotton gown around me, went to the locker room to get dressed and went home with my mom. I collapsed on my bed, curled up with the stuffed Koala bear the nuns from my high school had given me, and slept.

⌢

Almost two years after I'd finished chemotherapy for breast cancer, I returned to those memories, questioning whether they were real or imagined. I knew the tattoos were real, but everything else? Did the tattoos hurt that much? Was the table as cold and hard as I recalled? Did my mother keep telling me to stay still? Did I see a red laser light?

And, importantly, was the procedure even done anymore? I'd met and spoken with plenty of other cancer patients, including those who have had radiation: the topic of tattoos never came up. In the decades since I received my tattoos, had the medical brain trust come up with a better solution for guiding beams of radiation than marking patients with indelible ink?

When my curiosity got the best of me, I did an Internet search and found a patient information document, *Radiation Therapy to the Breast or Chest Wall*, on Memorial Sloan Kettering's website. What I'd remembered on my first day of chemo was my first day at Memorial Sloan Kettering—but it wasn't the first day of radiation therapy. It was my *simulation*—the trial run before treatment starts.

That document confirmed my memories of being cold and topless on a hard table. It confirmed the red laser beams and that I had to stay still for a long time. It also described the feeling of getting a tattoo as a *pinprick*.

Over thirty years later, it's still done this way. No wonder no one ever wants to talk about it.

⌐⌐

As the Benadryl wore off, I sensed a presence near me. I opened my eyes. A nurse was changing my medications.

"How are you feeling?"

"Groggy and cold," I answered, wondering whether I felt cold because it was cold or because I'd revisited all those memories.

"I'll get you a blanket," she said.

A moment later she tucked the blanket around me like my mom would have done. Its warmth surrounded and calmed me.

"Do you want anything else? How about some water?"

"That would be great, thanks."

I sipped the water, snuggled under the blanket, and began to doze again. Some hours later, I woke a little after 3:00 p.m. The boys would be home from school by now. All the patients who had started the day with me—the young man and the woman with the pink lipstick—had left. I wanted to go home, but I still had a couple of hours to go.

As I started to feel sorry for myself, an older woman sporting a white turban and fantastic silver hoop earrings walked into the infusion room and made her way toward me. She asked if the chair next to mine was taken.

"It's all yours," I said.

"It's your first day, isn't it?" she asked before she settled in.

"Yes."

"I have breast cancer," she said, collapsing into the chair and arranging her ample hips within it. Then she raised the footrest.

"So do I."

"Do you mind if I take off my turban? I'm so hot," she said, fanning her face.

"Not at all."

"Excuse me, everyone," the woman announced to the room, "I'm taking off my turban. I have no hair. If that's a problem for you, tell me now."

I wasn't sure why she felt the need to explain that to this captive audience. It went with the territory, as far as I could tell.

⌒

All of humanity sat in this room with me—the old and young, men and women, all races, ethnicities, and backgrounds.

I watched an older woman sleep while her daughter held her hand during those long afternoons.

I sat next to a young woman who was a distance runner. She wore her race shirts to treatment.

On some days, a friend whose son swam with Katie and with whom I'd spent many hours poolside joined me. He was in treatment too.

⌒

As I moved through the months, I began writing about the people I met in a journal Katie gave me, along with a card that read, "Mom, I know you're not thrilled with how long you have to spend at the hospital. Maybe this journal can pass the time more quickly."

And it did. I wrote about the other patients, my doctors, nurses, and friends. I also wrote about the many kindnesses I received. I wrote and cried and cried and wrote. I poured myself into that notebook—the bitter and the sweet, all worthy of tears.

⌒

Thirty-five years earlier, in a black and white composition notebook that I wished I'd saved, I wrote about the patients, doctors, and nurses I encountered during the months of radiation therapy.

What was I trying to understand then? Perhaps I understood, but couldn't articulate, that cancer's grasp doesn't discriminate.

I know this now: Cancer is an equal opportunity disease. Tara Williamson, an internationally recognized, certified areola complex, 3D nipple and scar camouflage tattoo artist, breast cancer survivor, nurse, advocate, and owner of Pink Ink Tattoo, explained it to me this way: "Cancer is incredibly humanizing. No one is immune, and we're all the same when it hits."

⌒

I turned to my notebook but couldn't concentrate. I decided to watch *Downton Abbey* instead. At least with my headphones on, lost in the distant elegance of Edwardian England, I wouldn't hear the infusion pumps' constant pinging alarms, letting the nurses know that someone's medication needed attention.

Athena texted and promised to bring me homemade dumplings and spring rolls that evening. Lucky me!

*Don't get spoiled. I'm not making these every time, okay?* she added to her text.

*Not that I'd expect you to, but thanks, sweetie!* I texted her back.

Except she did make them, almost every time I had treatment. When nothing else tasted good, Athena's dishes were always delicious.

Toward the end of the afternoon, a nurse handed me a sheet listing my appointments for the next three weeks, then explained I had to come to the office the next day for a Neulasta shot.

"What, pray tell, is a Neulasta shot?" I asked her.

"It's a medication that helps prevent infection. Make sure you take Claritin and Advil tonight, tomorrow morning and evening, and Saturday morning. That should help with any bone pain."

"Bone pain? What's bone pain?" I asked.

"You'll know it when you feel it."

"That sounds like the Supreme Court's definition of obscenity, you know it when you see it."

The nurse gave me a sidelong glance.

"But I can't take Advil. I'm allergic," I continued.

"Well, take the Claritin. Hopefully, that'll work. Most people don't have any problem. Do you still have the little bag from this morning? There should be another package in it."

I dug around in my backpack, pulled out a little box and handed it to the nurse. She explained that this was another anti-nausea medication, but in a patch. She stuck the patch on my upper arm and told me to wear it for a week.

My infusion pump started bleating. The nurse turned the pump off, removed the IV from my port, asked me my date of birth again—to confirm that an imposter didn't hijack my chemo session—and checked my blood pressure.

"You're done."

"Thanks," I replied, feeling the relief wash over me.

I fled from the office to the parking lot, happy to be moving, walking, and breathing in fresh air. I jumped in my car, then texted Tim to let him know that I was on my way. I drove home as fast as I could, which in rush hour traffic on I-287 wasn't all that fast, but it was still away from the infusion room.

One down, five to go.

⌒

# The Practical Reality
**Advice-Giving From Those of You Who Haven't Gone Through It or Aren't Versed in It**

To all the family, friends, and strangers who feel compelled to give advice to newly diagnosed cancer patients, cancer patients in treatment, or cancer survivors, please consider the following before you open your mouth:

Are you a doctor, nurse, or other health care professional with specialized training in oncology? If yes, go to question two. If not, zip it.

Are you a doctor, nurse, or other health care professional with specialized training in oncology and currently caring for *this patient*? If yes, give all the advice your patient asks you for. If not, zip it.

If these parameters seem restrictive, they are for good reason. I was stunned at what friends and strangers said to me after my diagnosis. Here are some examples:

Example One:

About a month into chemotherapy, I was at the grocery store wearing my scarf to cover my hair loss when I met another woman from my town.

"Hey Chris, I haven't seen you in a while. Oh my gosh, what happened to your hair?"

The friend stood there with her mouth wide-open.

"Well, I have breast cancer and am in chemotherapy right now."

"I'm sorry. My aunt had breast cancer too. She died a few years ago."

*Thanks.*

Example Two:

A few months into treatment, walking my dog, I passed a neighbor who was taking her recycling cans in from the curb.

"Hi, Chris. I'm so sorry about what you're going through."

"Thanks. I appreciate it."

"But look at the bright side, at least you're getting a free boob job. Are you getting the implants, or the surgery with the tummy tuck too?"

"I'll be having a bilateral mastectomy with implant reconstruction."

"My girlfriend had breast cancer and she told me that the implants are the best."

*Oh God.*

Example Three:

As I recovered from chemotherapy and before my surgery, I rested in the shade at a local pool as James swam and played with his friends. Another family's nanny sat down next to me and whispered, "Can I talk to you?"

"Sure. What's up?"

"Does it, um, run in your family?"

"What? Do you mean cancer? I had genetic testing done. I have no genetic predisposition for breast, ovarian, or uterine cancer."

"Have you seen the series *The Truth About Cancer*?"

"I've heard about it. That's not my thing. I have great docs, and I trust them."

"What about your diet? Have you ever tried turmeric tea? It has great cancer-fighting properties."

"Thanks," I replied and picked up my book.

*Geez. That's the kind I hate the most.*

⌒

Now, some of you who read this may shake your heads and think that there's no way these conversations happened. *Yes, way.* They did, and they do with far too much frequency. Individuals with cancer deal with similar conversations all the time because cancer is scary, difficult, and there's no rhyme or reason as to why some people get it. And, many people—even our closest friends and relatives—don't know what to say. I found they often acted or spoke before they thought, not out of malice or ill will, but in their nervousness and fear. There is no one *right* thing to say. But there are plenty of awful things not to say.

For years, a poster has hung above my desk with words from the writer, Fran Lebowitz: "Think before you speak. Read before you think." In my view, the same rule should apply to cancer conversations. I say instead of offering advice, silver linings, or quests for a cause, simply connect with those friends or family members: they're the same people they've always been. Tell them that you care about them. Acknowledge that what they're dealing with must be terribly hard. Tell them you'll support them in whatever way they need.

Or, if doing is more your thing, offer meals or a meal delivery from a favorite restaurant, transportation to treatment, help with household chores, or an outing for coffee (then follow through).

**Having a *Go-To* Answer**

After being on the receiving end of too many difficult cancer conversations, I came up with a neutral, yet firm, response to deal with the many advice givers, however well-meaning their intent. It went something like this:

Thank you for your concern. I've put together a terrific team of doctors and other medical professionals whom I trust. I'm relying on their expertise to guide me in making these important decisions during this very stressful time in my life. But I'd love to hear about what you're reading now, or what your favorite Netflix show is. I'll have a lot of down time in the next few months.

This allowed me to be polite and set my boundaries and get some great Netflix recommendations, like *The Crown, Call the Midwife,* and *Outlander.*

Don't be afraid to craft your own individualized go-to answer. Then, practice saying it so you can use it when a friend, relative, or stranger offers advice that you don't need or want.

**Inspiration**

During treatment, friends and family members often told me how *inspiring, brave* and *how much of a fighter* I was. But I didn't feel like any of those things most of the time: I was scared, anxious, and unhappy. Instead of making assumptions about the emotional state of individuals with cancer, tell them how they *appear* to be handling they're situation with strength, grace, or good humor—whatever fits or describes them. Then, let them talk about how they actually feel.

## Music or Other Distractions

For cancer patients, listening to music is a fabulous distraction from all the waiting we have to do: we wait for appointments, wait for labs, wait for hours as infusions drip slowly into us, wait for radiation therapy, and so on and so on. One of my friends, a lymphoma survivor, made a playlist of her favorite 80's dance music and listened to it before every scan or treatment because it made her feel good. I did something similar, although my playlists were mash-ups of my favorite 70's classic rock artists, 80's alternative, and electronic dance music.

For me, reading was my go-to distraction more than music. During my cancer treatment, I stuck to lighter books: historical fiction, gardening books, some memoir, and comedy.

## Ribbons: Not Everyone Loves Them

This may surprise some folks, but not everyone loves awareness ribbons, pink or otherwise. Some patients love them and take inspiration from them, but others don't. Be aware and have a conversation before you go out and spend your cash on beribboned shirts, pins, hats, bracelets, or socks. Make sure the person you're buying for is cool with the ribbon thing.

## Soothing Socks

Hospitals, doctors' offices, examination rooms, infusion centers, and radiation therapy treatment rooms are cold, cold places. I don't like being cold. I like having cold feet even less. So, I looked for warm comfortable socks to wear when I was in treatment.

I loved the soft, aloe-infused socks that friends gave me. In addition to being warm, they helped my dry skin. A friend and survivor loved *Note to Self* socks, which have uplifting messages on them.

# Chapter 9
## To the Bone

To Do (3/16-4/16)
Talk Dr. Abbasi out of Neulasta shot
Keep life normal
Fail at both

OVERJOYED THE FIRST LONG day of treatment was over, I walked into the kitchen and felt its warmth surround me. My whole being sighed as if I'd held my breath all day. The late afternoon sun filled the kitchen with soft light, its glow in stark contrast to the infusion room's institutional lighting. I offered a silent benediction.

A vase of my favorite white lilies and pink roses from Kevin and Lina, my brother- and sister-in-law, was waiting for me with a note: *Go kick cancer's ass. We love you.*

I smiled, lowered my nose into the lilies, and inhaled. Their sweet perfume eased the memory of that awful chemical-scented air.

"Gorgeous," I whispered and smelled them again. I felt the tension release in my neck and shoulders.

James came in from the dining room where he was doing his homework and wrapped his arms around me. I kissed the top of his head, tousled his hair, and asked him about his day. As he often did, James declared school to be *boring*, except for recess, and filled me in on the kickball battle *du jour*. The fifth graders at his school lived for kickball, as the end-of-the-year tournament gave the victorious homeroom bragging rights to take to middle school.

"I know kickball rules the school, honey, but what about homework? Are you done? Need any help?"

"I'm almost done, and don't need any help. But what did you do today, Mom?"

"Honestly, James. I didn't do much, other than sit around, reading and napping."

"You took a nap? You never nap, Mom."

"Crazy, right? Some of the medicine made me very sleepy."

James looked up at me with his eyebrows knit together. I gave him a squeeze around the shoulders.

"Homework. Go finish," I said, and James returned to his books.

I glanced over at the stove where stacks of catering trays rested along with a card from Tim's partners: *Many prayers being sent your way for strength and grace. Hope this meal helps.* Tears welled up in my eyes. I turned and looked out the kitchen window.

Tim walked in the kitchen from his home office, pulled me into a hug, and kissed me. "I'm glad you're home," he said.

"What's with all this food? We'll never eat all this," I said, overwhelmed by the generosity.

"Yeah, I know. My office went a little overboard," Tim replied.

"Well, it's nice they sent dinner for the next week," I laughed.

I explained to Tim that I had to receive a Neulasta injection the following day. Neulasta counteracted chemotherapy's destruction of white blood cells, which can make patients prone to infection. The drug triggered the growth of white blood cells deep in the marrow of large bones like the thighs, hips, and back. With their growth also came an inflammatory response, which was why taking Advil and Claritin helped alleviate the pain. Tim looked wary and reminded me that I couldn't take Advil. I tried reassuring him.

"I'll take the Claritin and see how it goes. The nurse said that most people tolerate the injection well."

I smiled. He frowned.

"I'm starving," I went on. "So let's heat up the dumplings and spring rolls for a nosh."

An hour or so later, Tim, the boys, and I sat around the kitchen table having dinner. It could have been any other night if I'd made dinner, or if the uncertainty of what was to come didn't loom over us.

I tried asking Tom about his day. He didn't have much to say. Tom dug into the pasta and poked at everything else. I asked him if there was anything wrong.

"Is it going to be like this every week?" Tom answered my question with his.

"Like what?"

"With you not cooking and everything?"

"Oh, Tom," I sighed. "People have offered to help with meals on my treatment days because I won't be home all day."

"But it's not the same . . ."

"I know, but . . . it's only once every three weeks."

"I guess," he mumbled and pushed his chair back. He scraped his plate into the trash and said he had to finish his homework. James jumped up and said he wanted to take a shower, leaving Tim and me alone at the table.

"What was that about?" I asked.

"I think the boys are confused and scared. No one really knew what to expect today," Tim said as he reached over and took my hand.

We sat in silence. Like kids, my cancer diagnosis didn't come with an instruction manual. We'd have to figure it out as we went along.

As Tim and I started clearing the dishes, I had an idea. I suggested to Tim that we go someplace warm for a few days before my next infusion, as the boys were on spring break. We could use a change of scenery. Tim agreed.

"How about the Keys? Tom loved it when he went sailing there with the Boy Scouts last year. Ever since we saw his pictures of that crystal blue water, we've wanted to go," Tim said.

I agreed, then texted Dr. Abbasi to see if he had any objection to the trip. He didn't. I quickly checked flight prices, then headed to bed, feeling content that I had a trip to plan and that we'd all have something to look forward too.

The following morning, I woke up with so much energy. I got the boys up, took the Claritin, started laundry, made lunches, dropped off the boys at school, and went to spin class.

I didn't know that I was in the middle of steroid-induced rush and would crash hard before the day ended.

By the time I arrived home after getting the Neulasta injection, Tim had picked up the boys, who were ready for the weekend away. I collapsed into the chair at my desk.

"How was the shot?" Tim asked as he walked into the kitchen. "Are you okay? You look pale."

"The shot was fine, but I feel a little queasy and so tired all of a sudden. I have to take the anti-nausea medication. Can you grab it for me? It's upstairs."

Tim brought me the brown prescription bottle filled with little white pills. I swallowed one with some water.

"Ugh. This tastes so weird," I said. "Tim, taste my water."

"What?"

"Taste it. Tell me if it tastes right."

He took a swig.

"It's water, Chris. It's fine."

"No, it's not fine. It tastes like metal. This cannot be starting already. Come on."

"What's starting?"

"Side effects. Remember? My sense of taste may change. Shit. What am I going to drink?"

"We'll find a different bottled water that doesn't taste weird to you. We'll figure it out," Tim replied.

I didn't feel like eating, so I decided to go to bed and skip dinner. Tim looked drawn, the shadows under his eyes dark, as I kissed him goodnight.

"Please try not to worry. I'm sure I'll feel better in the morning."

I wasn't better in the morning, or the morning after that, or the morning after that. When I woke up, I felt like I had a bad cold or the flu, with that aching feeling in my thighs. *I'd know it when I felt it: Bone pain.*

The bone pain was the worst part of going through chemotherapy, all of which was awful.

The bone pain was worse than losing my hair.

The bone pain was worse than the weird metal taste in my mouth.

The bone pain was worse than my tearing eyes.

The bone pain was worse than the blistering rash I had on my hands, arms, and feet.

The only thing rivaling the bone pain in its awfulness was the diarrhea accompanying each infusion, notwithstanding that I popped Imodium pills like M&M's.

After each injection, I held out hope that Claritin alone would work to prevent the bone pain. It didn't. The bone pain was like having a root-canal-worthy toothache in my thighs. Nothing touched this pain—not Tylenol, not heat, not muscle relaxers.

As quickly as it showed up, the pain would disappear after three days. Neulasta did what it was supposed to do, and my white counts stayed normal through treatment.

But during those three days, my life stood still. The pain consumed and exhausted me. I lost myself. I couldn't think of anything other than the pain and when it would end. I couldn't read. I couldn't make a cup of tea or get dinner ready.

Through it all, Ollie never left me. Ollie had been my dog first, from the time when we first brought him home as a puppy, notwithstanding the kids' insistence that they'd take care of him. I'd never had a dog while growing up, and I learned how loyal they are during my year with the Beast. When I dozed in my family room in my favorite chair, Ollie sat on the ottoman next to me and rested his head on my sore legs—as if he knew and did what he could to make me feel better.

With Ollie at my side, I watched my garden slowly come to life through the windows, as I had neither the energy nor the inclination to go outside and work. Any other year, I would have pruned and planted. My shears would have never been far from my hands. I would have gone to the nursery and chosen bright yellow and tangerine-colored pansies for the urns on the patio. I would have hung the chimes and welcomed their sonorous song on the breeze. I would have cleaned out the fountain, filled it with fresh water and arranged the dark river rocks around it.

Not that year. I'd retreated so far into myself that none of it mattered. I left the dead, brown greens from the holidays in the urns. Why should I undertake such a Herculean effort to dig them out, compost them, and plant anew? The pansies were going to bloom and die anyway. All I wanted to do was sleep—but sleep wasn't much of a mercy either. Most of those nights I half-dozed and imagined or dreamed little colonies of white blood cells growing deep inside my bones, like barnacles on a pier. The tears streamed down my face as wave after wave of pain rolled up and down my thighs. I lay awake furious that I couldn't sleep, and Tim could. Exhausted, I reached for my mom's rosary on my bedside table and began the cycle of prayers until I finally slept.

The pain tested me more than anything else because I couldn't control it. I couldn't alleviate it, unlike most of the other side effects. I felt so helpless and frustrated that this incredible, life-saving drug caused such agony. I railed again the unfairness of it all.

If I only I could take Advil, I wouldn't be in pain.

If only I didn't have cancer as a kid, I wouldn't have cancer today.

If only I didn't have cancer at all.

During those helpless bone-pain days, my mind often returned to my earlier years with cancer, when I felt especially helpless as a fourteen-year-old.

⟶

I went alone into the cold radiation therapy room where the large, green linear accelerator lived. I named it, *the Zapper*.

I'd lay on a hard table, topless and shivering, while the technician would adjust the machine's settings to direct the photon beams guided by the tattoos on my body, then leave. As I listened to the Zapper whir, buzz, and groan, I'd keep my fear at bay by counting from one to ten over and over in my head.

I received radiation to the neck, chest and armpits.

At first, I didn't feel any different: I could still eat, function, and complete my school readings and assignments each day. Even though my teachers decided I wouldn't be graded during the first quarter, I didn't want to be too far behind when I returned to school full-time. I went to school once a week, handed in my work, and caught up with friends and forensics. One day a week, I felt like a regular teenager and happy.

As the September passed into October, the radiation site shifted to my abdomen—and everything changed. After each treatment, I became nauseous even before I left the locker room. I'd get in the car and lay in the backseat, hoping I wouldn't get sick. But I did. I had a basin with me in the car that I heaved into day after day.

I couldn't bear the thought of eating. I lost weight, about fifteen pounds. My postman-blue, gabardine A-line uniform skirt grew looser on me each time I wore it to school. By the time I finished treatment, I'd dropped two dress sizes and needed a new uniform skirt.

I felt so powerless during those days. I swore to myself that once it was over, I wouldn't look back. I never wanted to feel that I had no control over my life again. When I was at my worst, my mom often would urge me to *hang on* and remind me that it would be over soon.

While her words didn't console me, they made me push through.

⌣

I would have never imagined then that I'd have to do it again thirty-five years later. Yet, while curled in my chair in the family room trying to ignore the pain in my thighs, I'd count down each day and urge myself to hang on.

*For three days.*

*For two days.*

*Only one more day, Christine. You can do anything for one day.*

⌣

Because Neulasta caused me such grief, I decided to go to the one person who could end my personal hell: Dr. Abbasi. Starting with the second injection, I tried to talk him out of it (as I tried each cycle thereafter, ever hopeful).

I smiled my brightest smile at him and said, "Dr. Abbasi, since I'm doing so well, and my counts are so good, let's skip the Neulasta this time so I can avoid the bone pain. It's awful, just so you know."

"Yes, I know. Many patients say this. This side effect can be worse than the chemo," he acknowledged.

"So, we can skip the shot, then?" I asked hopefully.

With one finger on his moustache and one on his cheek, Dr. Abbasi looked at his computer. He paused long enough to make me feel like he was considering my request, (when it wasn't even a real possibility.) Then he turned toward me, ran his hand over his temple, and said, "You know, it would be better for you if we did the Neulasta."

This, he said every single time.

So *we* did the injection.

Bone pain or not, Dr. Spine of Steel wouldn't budge.

⌣

I could have declined the injections—I was an adult, after all, and I had choices. Yet I understood the risks of not receiving the injection and my ingrained sense of determination to push through held sway. But still, that didn't stop me from trying to get out of it.

What the hell was wrong with me? I was acting out in a way I'd never tolerate from my own kids, with a mess of poor attempts at negotiation, wheedling, and whining. It was almost as if I were fourteen again.

⌣

As I moved past the bone pain, I pushed the melancholy and anger from my mind. In those early months, I thought I did a fantastic job carrying on. I planned our trip to Florida. Meetings for the high school PTO and swim team, walks, and scouting events filled my calendar.

⌣

I didn't appreciate the profound disconnect between my perception and my family's of how I had managed my breast cancer. A year after I'd finished chemotherapy, I was working on an assignment for a writing class in which I had to describe a time when I wasn't at my best.

As I reflected on my behavior during the early bone pain days, I realized how much of a brat I had been.

I also had to write about other characters' points of view of that same time, so after offering my view that I had kept life as normal as possible for the family, I asked Tim what he remembered about the early months of treatment.

"Nothing was normal. Nothing. Yes, you did your best with the errands, activities, and volunteering. But there was always another doctor's appointment, or a lab visit, or a test. Cancer took over. The stress in the house was palpable. There were days I felt I could barely get through. You were sick and exhausted, and no one knew what to do for you when you were in pain. I was so afraid you'd die."

Tom echoed Tim's sentiments.

"I would describe the experience as pure shit. I didn't want to be around you with your porcupine head and dry scaly skin. You smelled awful, like chemicals, medication and fear. It reminded me of when Granddad was dying from cancer. You were a monster to me."

I blinked, shocked at his words and the vehemence with which he said them.

I turned away from Tom so he wouldn't see my face.

During that time, I'd become the Beast, and I hadn't known it.

That ugly truth cut me to the bone.

❧

## The Practical Reality
### Diet Tips

My oncologist didn't give me a specific diet to follow during chemotherapy, other than he didn't want me eating soy products because soy contains plant estrogens and I had estrogen receptor positive cancer. He also asked me to avoid raw fish—no oysters on the half shell or sushi, because one bad oyster or tuna roll and I'd get sick. His view generally was that I should eat whatever tasted good or didn't taste terrible because my sense of taste would change due to the chemotherapy drugs I was on. However, your doctor may have a different view. Follow your own doctor's advice.

While I was in treatment, I tried to eat a balanced, healthy diet, like I normally did: plenty of water, vegetables and fruit, multi-grains, and whatever proteins I liked. For me, those proteins were eggs, plain low-fat yogurt, and chicken. Beef, fish, and sweet foods tasted off to me, probably because my mouth tasted like aluminum foil much of the time.

I am not a registered dietician, and there are plenty of good ones out there (please see *Resources*). Fortunately, there are hundreds of books about diet and cancer. One of my favorites was *Anticancer: A New Way of Life* by David Servan-Schreiber.

After I finished treatment, I saw an excellent dietician who fine-tuned my eating habits to follow a low sugar/anti-inflammatory diet. Did I cut out all sugar from my diet? No, I do enjoy a sweet treat every now and again. Did I stop drinking wine? No. Do I do it in moderation? Yes. Will I ever change my mind about kale? No.

I also fast twice a week because that works for me for weight loss and maintenance. But I recognize that choice is not for everyone.

We have to live in this life of ours. We have to eat. Talk to your doctor about diet and healthy eating. Figure out what works for you and your family. Figure out what brings you peace of mind in your diet and enjoy what's on your plate.

**Dry and Peeling Skin**

Shortly after I started chemotherapy, I noticed that the skin on my palms, arms, and feet started to blister and peel like I had a sunburn. Turns out I had hand-foot syndrome, also known in medical parlance as *palmar-plantar erythrodysesthesia* (I can't even say that). It's a side effect from chemotherapy that happens when a small amount of chemotherapy medications leak out of tiny blood vessels on the palms of the hands and soles of the feet. It's like getting a sunburn or chemical burn from the inside out, and it's gross to have skin peeling off your body.

To mitigate the peeling and dryness, my sister-in-law gifted me with organic skin care products from Osea Malibu, including Anti-

Aging Body Balm and Undaria Algae Oil. I loved the stuff. I also kept Udderly Smooth hand cream on my desk, bedside table, and in my car. I slathered myself with these moisturizers, and over time, the peeling and blistering stopped (please see *Resources*).

**Hydrate, Hydrate, Hydrate**

Sixty-four ounces of water a day, at a minimum, is what experts say we should drink for overall health.

I brought a full twenty-four-ounce insulated water bottle with me to treatment. I filled and drank it at least twice more over the many hours I spent in the infusion chair. I also drank flavored seltzer and had frozen juice pops (no sugar added) when I was tired of water.

Chemotherapy, radiation therapy and surgery—and their side effects (e.g. diarrhea, vomiting)—can be dehydrating. Dehydration occurs when an individual does not take in enough fluid or loses too much.

If nausea or vomiting is preventing you from drinking, contact your health care team for guidance.

**Mantra-Making**

One of my friends suggested that individuals living with cancer consider creating a mantra for themselves. A mantra is a simple, positive phrase that can be repeated in times of stress or anxiety or during scans. My friend's was, *I am healthy. I am strong. I will survive.* Even though she finished her treatment a few years ago, she still says it every morning to start her day on a positive note. Mine was, *The only way out is through.* Those words reminded me then (and now) that I could face anything as long as I kept going.

**Meditation**

Meditation is an approach to training the mind to encourage a heightened state of awareness and attention. Meditation has been practiced in cultures all over the world for thousands of years, and nearly every world religion, including Buddhism, Hinduism, Christianity, Judaism, and Islam, has a tradition of using meditative practices. In my Catholic tradition, to meditate, I pray the rosary as it involves the repetition of the same prayers in a cycle. I also learned to practice concentration and guided meditations through wellness programs in my oncologist's practice.

Concentration meditation involves focusing on something—whether it's the breath, a mantra, a candle flame, crystal, flower, or a repetitive sound like a gong—and tuning out the rest of the world. I learned that if a thought entered my mind, I would acknowledge it, then return my attention to the object. This was a great form of meditation for me, a beginner, because I could do it for a few minutes at a time.

I also participated in guided meditations where the teacher walked me (and the class) through the meditation step by step.

Over time, I found that meditation helped me to decrease my stress and anxiety and sleep better, particularly since I use the Insight Timer app that has thousands of free meditation programs (please see *Resources*).

**Neuropathy**

I have chemotherapy-induced peripheral neuropathy in my feet, a common side effect from the platinum and taxane chemotherapy that I received. In simple terms, peripheral neuropathy is damage to the nerves in the peripheral nervous system, which is made up of nerves that bring signals from the brain and spinal cord to other parts of the body, such as the hands and feet. The most common symptoms include:

- tingling, burning, weakness, or numbness in arms, hands, legs, and feet
- sudden, sharp, stabbing, or shocking pain
- loss of the sense of touch
- loss of balance
- loss of motor skills, such as having trouble picking up objects or fastening clothing

My neuropathy is the numbness/tingling kind and flares up if I spend a long day on my feet.

Breastcancer.org reported on a study suggesting that wearing frozen gloves or socks, called cryotherapy, for ninety minutes during Taxol treatment may help prevent neuropathy symptoms. It is unclear whether cryotherapy would benefit individuals treated with platinum chemotherapy medicines or with targeted treatments such as Perjeta, Ibrance or Kadcyla, which also cause neuropathy. Additional research in this area is ongoing.

In the meantime, if taxane chemotherapy is in your treatment plan, you may want to talk to your doctor about this study and whether wearing frozen socks and mittens during your infusion might make sense for you.

**Tissues**

After two cycles of chemotherapy, I noticed that my eyes starting tearing uncontrollably. When I asked my nurse about it, she told me it was a side effect of one of the chemotherapy drugs.

"That's why it's called *taxo-tear*. Get it?"

Terrible medical puns aside, she also told me that there was nothing I could do about the tears, other than carry lots of tissues. I made sure I had little packages or boxes of tissues with me, in my car, and on my desk.

# Chapter 10
## Angel in the Mailbox

To Do (4/16-5/16)
Florida!
Ditch wig
Bake cake
Say yes
Remember Jack

HAVING RECEIVED DR. ABBASI's blessing to get away, we headed to the Florida Keys for five days of sunshine. While Tim and I lounged by a pool, James and Tom swam for hours. I enjoyed the warmth of the sun and gazing across the brilliant blue water of the Atlantic. Being near the ocean always calmed my heart and mind. At Bahia Honda State Park, we walked along the beach with James, enjoying the warm green surf on our feet and picking up bits of coral and driftwood at the water's edge. The air was scented with salt, sunblock, and scrub pines. Tom went fishing for an afternoon, and one morning James swam with the dolphins. For the first time in many weeks, we felt relaxed. The change of scenery was exactly what we needed.

None of us wanted to go home to face more of my chemotherapy, but there was no choice. We got off the plane on a Wednesday night, and I headed to the infusion center the next morning.

⌒

By the time we returned home from Florida, my hair was falling out in clumps. A few days later, I went to my salon at 6:30 in the morning so Ricky, my hair stylist, could buzz my head before the rush of regulars arrived. If anyone met Ricky on the street, they might take in his tattoo-covered, body-builder-sized arms, bare head, and beard and think he designed custom motorcycles, rather than perfectly cut and styled hair for both women and men. I knew I wasn't the first of his clients to go through chemotherapy, and I wouldn't be the last. All of the salon's black leather and chrome chairs were empty, except for mine, and I appreciated his sensitivity and kindness to let me have this moment in privacy.

"Are you ready, sweetie? I won't buzz it all. I'm going to leave about an eighth of an inch. Hopefully, you'll keep that."

I nodded and watched in the big mirror as what was left of my beautiful brown hair fell to the floor. As I wiped the tears off my face, Ricky pulled me into a hug, wrapped his beefy arms around me as I rested my wet cheek on his chest.

I looked up, just as he wiped his own eyes, then looked down again.

I handed him the wig I'd bought at a store that he had recommended. The wig was similar to my original hair, dark brown, but a bit longer than my regular style. He adjusted it on my head and styled it. When he was finished, he cupped my chin with his hand and lifted it up. "Listen to me. You're going to get through this, and I'll be here waiting for you, for your next cut. Okay, baby?"

I nodded, looking directly into his warm, hazel eyes. "Thanks. You're the best. I'll be seeing you."

I walked out and wouldn't return for eight months.

⌒

A few weeks later, when the weather became warmer and more humid, the thought of wearing a hot, itchy wig became less appealing. I wore my Buff® scarves or a baseball cap during my daily walk with Ollie, and only wore the wig if I had to get dressed up.

One misty, gray morning, I saw my neighbor Shannon in the distance, running. I hadn't seen her in a couple of months. I dreaded the conversation I knew would take place when she saw my bald head, barely covered by the baseball cap I chose that morning.

Running down the incline in the road, Shannon stopped when she finally reached me.

"God, Chris, it's been a while," she said as she put both hands on her thighs and caught her breath. When she stood up and my almost-bald head registered, her expression dropped into a concerned frown.

"What is going on, Chris? What happened to your hair? Why do you look so pale . . .?"

Her voice trailed off as she pieced together the answer to her own questions. She gasped and covered her mouth with her hand.

"I'm sorry, Shannon, but I haven't told a lot of people about all this."

"Please, Chris! Don't be sorry. How are you holding up? How are Tim and the boys? What can I do to help?"

Her shock and concern touched me, and I quickly summarized the last two months for her, explaining why I had tried to keep the news on the down-low.

"It's been rough on the boys. Tom was upset more than I was about the hair. I have to go to doctor's every week, and it's wreaking havoc on the kids' schedules. They're not crazy about all the delivered food and changes to their routines. I'm tired a lot too."

"Well then, please give me something to do to help out—drive the kids, cook a meal, laundry, even clean your house. Just tell me, and it will be done."

"No, we really don't need any help, right now. I'm trying to keep everything as normal as possible for the kids. It's not that I don't appreciate the offer."

"There must be something you need." Shannon insisted.

"Honestly, Shannon, there isn't. Tim's office sends us meals on my treatment days. And Tim has been managing the boys for now."

Shannon placed her hands on my shoulders and gave me a gentle shake.

"Chris, please let me help. People want to help. Do you know why? Because it makes them feel good."

"I know but . . ." I looked away, not wanting her to see my tears.

"Let those of us who care about you, help."

I turned back to her and nodded slowly. My need to control my cancer—its progression, its outcome, and my emotions around it—had spread to walling off all support from friends. Yes, asking for help was a sign of vulnerability, but I couldn't keep going it alone.

"You're right, but it's hard for me to accept help even when I'm not sick," I sniffed, and we both laughed. "I guess I thought it would be better if I did it all on my own."

"You know I'm right," Shannon replied. "And you don't have to do it all on your own. I'll help with whatever you need."

"That would be great. When I have my surgery in a few months, I'll put you on the list for meals and rides. I won't be able to do much then."

With those words, I let out a sigh of relief.

As Ollie and I headed home, I shook my head at my lack of self-awareness. Shannon's words had rocked me. By holding tight to my perceived control and insisting on doing everything, I thought I could hang on to *normal*. In retrospect, I was alienating everyone around me, including my own family. I was pushing them away when they needed me as much as I needed them.

⌒

Later that day, I found a small gift bag in my mailbox with a note from Shannon attached.

"We swim moms have to stick together and help each other out. Here's my cell phone number. Call me anytime."

A necklace with a crystal pendant made to look like a little blue flower, embossed with a small angel, was inside the bag. *A guardian angel to watch over me,* I thought.

Shannon's honest words gave me the courage to loosen my grip. I decided to stop saying *No* and to start saying *Yes.*

"Yes, I would love to walk with you."

"Yes, I would love to have coffee."

"Yes, I would love to have company during my infusion."

I put the necklace on then and there, and from then on, wore it every day I was in treatment.

⌒

Within days of running into Shannon on our street, a karmic shift in my universe began as others' help, kindness, and generosity poured into my life.

Jeanne, my mother-in-law, who always called me the *daughter of her heart,* sent me a card with one word on it: *Grace.*

Mass cards and prayer cards from relatives and family friends arrived in the mail almost every day.

Tim came home from work with a pin blessed by Pope Francis and a note from one of his colleagues that read: *Please give this to Chris.*

A gift of a beautiful fleece shawl kept me warm during my infusions and a box of organic skin care products from my sister-in-law, Lina, helped with the dryness from the medications.

Soothing bath salts, another thoughtful present, eased my bone pain.

A pot of spaghetti Bolognese, hydrangeas for my garden, and a bracelet that said, *Be Brave*, all helped to give me hope and strength.

*Thinking of You* was the universal message with each gift, infusing my life with love, and lifting my spirits.

⌒⁀

My spirits rose even further after Dr. Abbasi reminded me that I would be halfway done with treatment in early May.

"We should celebrate," I said, smiling at him. "I'll bake you a cake."

"Maybe you should bake half a cake," he laughed at me.

"Who does that, Dr. Abbasi?" I replied, smirking back at him. "No one bakes half a cake. That's ridiculous."

To mark the day, I baked Dr. Abbasi the best damn cinnamon sour cream coffee cake I ever made from a recipe that had circulated among the families of the Oak Street Grammar School since 2005.

When I arrived for my next infusion, I gave the cake to one of the nurses to take to the break room and asked her to let Dr. Abbasi know it was there. I never knew if Dr. Abbasi had a slice, let alone half the cake, because only crumbs were left by the end of the day. Still, this small victory, this halfway milestone on my long, long road, made me smile.

In May, just past that halfway point, an ultrasound showed that my tumors had shrunk. The chemotherapy that filled my veins every three weeks was working. This brought me a measure of relief, but Dr. Abbasi reminded me of cancer's uncertainty when he told me we wouldn't really know anything until after the surgical pathology.

Despite his pragmatism, I took small comfort in Aunt Peg's notes that she sent each time I time I reached a new milestone, no matter how big or how small.

"I remember tracking mine: one-third through, one-half through, two-thirds through! Each step forward is one that becomes a step past."

Her notes were endearing. I saved every one of them.

The days and weeks leading to June settled into a steady rhythm. Each time I had another infusion, one of my friends or my sister sat with me, bringing coffee, my favorite blueberry scones from Starbucks, and wonderful, mindless magazines. We'd laugh over the crazy expensive clothes in the pages we'd never buy or wear and drool over the perfectly appointed houses.

I could have had any of the conversations and coffee at my favorite local lunch place and, truth be told, would have preferred that to having them in the infusion room at the Simon Center. Still, the friendship and company made those long infusion-filled days more bearable.

Other days, when I was alone in the center, friends and family flooded my email and lit up my phone with jokes, funny videos, and clips from their favorite comedians. Some made me snort out loud, which was like laughing in a library or at church. I had to ignore the stares from other chemo patients, who wondered what could possibly be so funny about where we were all sitting.

As I sat in the office waiting room for one of my lab visits, I saw the man whom I believed was Jack, the swim official. He looked more drawn than the last time I saw him. Before I had a chance to introduce myself to him, he said, "Excuse me, you look so familiar. Are any of your kids swimmers?"

"Yes, they are," I replied, offering my hand. "I'm Chris Corrigan. My daughter, Katie, and my son, Tom, are both swimmers. I've seen you at their Somerset Hills YMCA meets, right? You're Jack?"

"Yes, that's right. And now I remember you too, Chris! I've been dealing with health issues. Looks like you are too?"

"Yes, breast cancer."

"I'm done with my treatment, but it's left me very dehydrated, so I need to come in every so often for fluids. Please give everyone at the Y my regards."

"I will. We all want to see you back on deck soon."

Jack smiled a bright Irish smile at me at me, leaned his head back on the light wooden waiting room chair, and closed his eyes.

I saw him one or two more times after that, but never again at a swim meet.

⤙

A year later, an email from the swim team informed us that Jack had died. I put my head on my desk and sobbed. I had only just finished my own treatment, and this news crushed me. Cancer had forced me to own the truth that most of us try to ignore until we can't: our time is limited.

I found Jack's obituary online, and as I read it, I tried to remember our conversations in the infusion center. I didn't know they would be the last ones we'd have. Shouldn't the universe let us know that somehow? Give us a signal? Prod us to pay attention so we can say more than ordinary small talk? It didn't, and it won't. We must infuse the mundane with meaning so our moments and memories aren't lost.

I thought of Jack whenever I worked at a swim meet. I haven't forgotten how much he loved the sport or how he was quick with a smile and could put even the youngest, most novice swimmers at ease before a race. Jack treated everyone fairly and kindly: swimmers, coaches, and parents.

If only life had been more kind to him.

⤙

By the end of spring, Tim had grown tired of the old, dead plants in our outdoor planters. On a warm Saturday, we drove to our favorite nursery to choose something fresh and bright to fill them in. Tim said he'd do all the work for me.

We walked through the nursery slowly because my thighs ached. Tim left me in the annuals section as he went to look for herbs and vegetables for his garden. As I looked at all the colorful petals, Amy, the manager, approached. Her mouth dropped open as she neared.

"Chris, Tim told us that you weren't well, but I had no idea you'd been so sick," she said, her voice trailing off.

"Yeah, well, as you can see," I threw my hands up and rolled my eyes as I gestured to the baseball cap hiding my bald head, "I'm going through chemo right now for breast cancer."

Shannon, Amy's cousin who also worked at the nursery, joined us.

"Oh Chris, I'm so sorry. How long is your treatment?" Shannon asked.

"I'll be done in July, and I'll have surgery in August after I recover from the chemo."

I quickly changed the subject, pointing to a table of summer annuals. "I'm not up to a lot of gardening right now but would love flowers for my planters."

"Let us do the planters, Chris. Please," Amy said.

"Tell us what colors you like, and we'll come out and plant them for you. It's the least we can do," Shannon added.

I hesitated in the face of such a generous offer. I reached up and rubbed my angel pendent and asked, "Are you sure? It's a lot of planters."

"Please let us do this for you," Amy replied.

"Okay. Thank you, Amy. That's so kind."

Amy and Shannon helped me choose flowers in pink and yellow, blue and white—my favorite seasonal colors.

The next day, the nursery's crew showed up and filled our urns with the lantana, bright pink geraniums, and petunias. They lit up my entryway and patio, reminding me that help and kindness were waiting as long as I had the courage and humility to accept them.

## The Practical Reality

### Exercise

Remember the Nike slogan, *Just Do It?* For cancer patients, I think the slogan should say, *Just Do Something*, assuming your health care team is on board and okay with whatever exercise routine you choose to adopt.

For me, circuit weight training twice a week helped maintain my upper body strength and ensured I was as strong as I could be going into my surgery. While I was in treatment, I walked one to three miles every day depending on my fatigue and energy level. Exercise helped get me out of my head and out of my house because cancer can be isolating. Exercising helped me maintain a level of normalcy when I felt anything but normal.

### Eyebrows and Lashes

When I learned I would lose my hair from chemotherapy, I focused on my head and not on all the other places I had hair—on the upside, no shaving, no waxing, no problem! Before cancer, I had thick brows and lashes. I never needed to use a brow pencil, and one coat of mascara was more than enough. Although I didn't lose all of my brows or lashes, they thinned considerably. So what to do about this?

There are a couple of options for eyebrows, with the easiest and least expensive being to use an eyebrow pencil or eyebrow palette. I use a mineral powder eyebrow palette almost every day to fill in my brows. Another option is micro-blading, a semi-permanent makeup treatment that fills in thin or sparse eyebrows through a hand-held tool that uses needles to apply special pigments under the top layer of the skin to simulate the look of eyebrow hairs.

Eyelashes are trickier. As of this writing, there is one FDA-approved prescription serum for eyelash regrowth. Another option is eyelash extensions, although individuals without any lashes left cannot use extensions.

In addition, many cosmetic companies manufacture eyelash

or eyebrow serums that may condition or promote thickening of eyebrows and lashes; however, their efficacy depends on the individual.

## Isolation

Cancer isolated me. Some days, I felt physically awful and didn't have the energy to engage. Some days, I looked awful and didn't want others to see me. Some days, I felt like no one else *got* what I was going through. However, I found spending time with my supportive friends and family helped to keep the fear, anxiety, or moodiness at bay.

Also, my support groups—whether in person, through social media platforms, or by phone—were a great way to engage with others who are or have been through a similar cancer. After I attended a support group meeting or posted a question or comment online, more often than not, I felt better than I did when I walked in or was sitting alone noodling over something that was bothering me.

## Silk Pillowcases

Hair loss due to cancer treatment is a real pain in the head. This was surprising to me. I knew I'd lose my hair, but I didn't know how irritating hair loss was. Silk or satin pillowcases helped to minimize my scalp irritation and hair loss because the fabric doesn't pull on the already weakened strands of hair and are softer to sleep on once all the hair is gone. They are available online, and at most department stores and home goods retailers.

# Chapter 11

## Light in Darkness

To Do (5/1-6/13)
Nap
Celebrate
Have topless photo shoot

As May progressed into June, I grew weak. Neulasta shots and months of bone pain notwithstanding, I came down with pneumonia with its teeth-chattering, bone-shaking chills, and raging fevers. The fatigue promised on my first day of treatment three months earlier crushed my body, mind, and soul.

I stole sleep in my car while waiting to pick up the boys. I slept on a chaise lounge at our pool club when I could no longer manage conversation with my friends. I slept in the family room, curled in my chair or sprawled on the leather sofa every afternoon so I would have some energy to finish out the day. I slept in waiting rooms at doctor appointments. I slept while Tim drove. But I never felt rested.

The effects of chemotherapy were as annihilating to me now as the effects of radiation were three decades earlier.

⌒

By the time I turned fifteen in late October 1981—after I was no longer vomiting every day—fatigue continued to flatten my world. I didn't have the energy to do my schoolwork, and my mom wouldn't let me go to school anymore. I traveled between my white and red bedroom under the eaves of our house on Staten Island, to the cold, green-tiled radiation therapy rooms at Memorial Sloan Kettering in New York, and back.

I spent afternoons dozing and listening to Stevie Nicks' *Bella Donna* album on my stereo. When one side ended, I'd crawl to the foot of my white, four-poster bed, reach down to the stereo on the floor, and flip the album to the other side. When that was too much effort, I'd lie on my red shag rug with my head propped up on a floor pillow and listen to the stereo while wrapped in my patchwork quilt. I was frustrated I couldn't be in school with my friends, but also too exhausted to even think about going to forensics tournaments or working on our school plays.

As shadows moved across my bedroom ceiling, I'd stare at the *Bella Donna* album cover, thinking Stevie Nicks was the coolest and most beautiful woman I'd ever seen, with her long hair, flowers, velvet boots, and flowing skirts. I was jealous that she got to live such a glamorous life, and I was trapped in my bedroom.

In my senior year of high school, every member of the graduating class included a favorite song as part of our yearbook entries. Mine was *Edge of Seventeen*, my hat-tip to Stevie's companionship during those dark, cold, lonely days a few years before.

⌒

Unlike the isolation I endured as a teenage cancer patient, my everyday life as an adult didn't stop because I had breast cancer. The early summer months of 2016 brought with them family celebrations. Although I attended, sang *Happy Birthday*, clapped for the fifth-grade graduates, and ate cake, I often felt detached. It was as though I were watching the action from the other side of a glass wall, with the sounds of celebration, the congratulations, and birthday wishes muffled, and the goofy fifth-graders out of reach.

Others looked at ease in conversation—probably talking about their jobs or latest projects, vacation plans, tennis matches, or rounds of golf. But as soon as I approached, those conversations paused and shifted to cancer. How much longer would I be in treatment? How I was managing my side effects? When I would have my surgery? While I smiled and answered their questions, part of me wanted to scream, "There's more to talk about than cancer!"

The conversations left me exhausted and filled with envy and bitterness. Their lives hadn't been cleaved in two. They didn't have a before and after. I did, and I couldn't push those feelings aside. They clung to me like a leech bleeding my spirit.

⁓

Thinking back to those events and my reactions to them, I realized how much perspective I'd lost. Other family members and friends were enduring their own losses, heartache, and pain. But the Beast had blinded me to all but what was in front of me at the moment:

The next treatment.

The next injection.

The next lab visit.

The next doctor's appointment.

⁓

Two years later, at one of my routine post-treatment check-ups, Dr. Abbasi asked me if a medical resident could sit in. I never had a problem with residents, physician assistant students, or nursing students listening to our conversations. I went to a teaching hospital and grew up in a home where healthcare ruled. I would have felt disloyal to object to having a *baby doc*, as my mom used to call the residents, at the appointment.

During my check-up, Dr. Abbasi asked me how my writing was going, and I gave him copies of essays that I'd published. He told the resident I'd started writing while I was in treatment and then continued afterwards. As the visit came to end, he explained to the resident that being a patient in treatment is like being in a tunnel at the back of a long train. The patient can't see the light at the end or the beautiful scenery to come. The doctors must remind their patients about the light.

Dr. Abbasi was like a lighthouse to me while I was in treatment, just as Stevie Nicks' music had been decades earlier. He helped me stay the course over and over, even when I wanted to jump off the train or get out of the boat. He kept me moving toward the light, moving toward a safe harbor through the whole long year, with his calm, steady presence.

⌒

Long before I had any of those insights, and while I was at my mother-in-law, Jeanne's, seventy-fifth birthday party two years earlier, I needed to escape from the country club ballroom with its chintz, crisp linens, heavy silver, well-meaning relatives, and their frustrating cancer questions. I made my way outside to the porch covered by a bright green and white awning. As I savored the quiet broken only by the periodic *ping!* of a club striking a ball, I shut my eyes for a moment, then was startled to hear, "Aunt Chris, is it true you have no hair under that wig?"

I opened my eyes to find Bella, my seven-year-old niece, standing in front of me.

I patted to a spot on the sofa next to me. She sat down and curled up against me. I rested my arm around her and replied, "Yes, Bella, it's true."

After a few minutes, Bella sat up and turned toward me. "Why don't you have any hair, Aunt Chris?"

"Well, sweetie, I'm sick and have to take special medicine to get better. Unfortunately, it made my hair fall out."

"You have cancer. You're sick like Grandad was."

"I do have cancer. It's a different kind than Grandad had though, Bella."

She was silent while trying to process this information.

"Are you going to keep wearing that wig?"

"I'll tell you a secret, Bella. I don't always wear the wig. Sometimes, I wear a baseball cap or a headband. I don't like the wig much."

"I don't either, Aunt Chris. It doesn't look like the old you."

Bella knitted her brows for a moment, turned to me, and suggested that I take off the wig. I laughed. That surely would have changed the tenor of the birthday party!

I leaned over and placed my hand on her cheek.

"I guess I could, but I don't think that's such a good idea right now. Maybe, we should go in and see if lunch is ready."

Bella put her arms around my neck and gave me a hug.

"I love you, Aunt Chris, and I'm sorry about your hair."

"Oh Bella, you made my heart sing," I said.

"How does your heart sing? Hearts can't sing, can they? They don't have mouths."

I laughed. "You're right. They can't. What I meant was you made me happy."

She took my hand, her small palm warm against mine, and the two of us went in for lunch.

Even in darkness, we still can enjoy moments of light and joy.

⌣

When I decided months earlier to have a bilateral mastectomy, I didn't think too much about it. My boobs were trying to kill me, and they needed to go. They had done their job, and I wasn't having any more children. I could let them go and have reconstruction, even though I knew I would lose one of my sexual hot spots in the process. But that didn't matter much by June of 2016, since Tim and I were well-nigh into the year of the drought.

There were no more easy, early mornings tangled in the sheets, Tim's hand on my hip, the rise and fall of his chest under my cheek. I couldn't bear the thought of sex, not when I looked as I did, not when I felt so little like the woman I'd been. My passion shriveled, as parched as my ravaged skin. I cringed from Tim's touch. I cocooned into myself.

*Don't look at me. Don't touch me. Please don't. And, I'm sorry and love you so. But, I can't. I simply can't.*

During our wedding, our priest told us that marriage required courage, extraordinary courage, in addition to love. I'd never forgotten those words, though I didn't understand what they meant then. Now Tim and I were deep into the courageous. I tested our vows that year, and Tim rarely complained. Rather, he held tight to me no matter how much I pushed him away. He reminded me that I was still beautiful to him. Each time he said those words and wiped my tears away, he brought me back to the light, back to our love.

—

As June moved toward July and my final chemotherapy treatment, I focused on the surgery to come at the end of the summer. I knew Dr. Diehl would perform the mastectomy, but I still needed to find a plastic surgeon for the reconstruction. After receiving several recommendations, I decided to meet with Dr. Rafizadeh.

Dr. Rafizadeh came out to the waiting room to greet me. He smiled, extended his hand, and introduced himself. His voice carried the slightest trace of an accent. *French maybe?* He was about six feet tall, with warm olive-toned skin and light brown eyes—a handsome man.

He led me to his paneled office. I noticed beautifully rendered drawings of the human form hanging on his office walls. Not surprisingly, he had an art background and would approach reconstruction with an artist's eye. For an art lover like myself, this put me immediately at ease.

He reviewed all of the options for breast and nipple reconstruction. He showed me the various implants. He explained the anatomy and made drawings so I understood exactly what would happen. I appreciated his patience.

After the lecture and sketches were over, we moved to the exam room. Dr. Rafizadeh asked me to change so that he could take some photographs and do an exam.

*Photographs? Of me, topless? Sweet Jesus. The dude's standing there with a digital camera.*

I had a hard time wrapping my head around baring my boobs for a photograph, even though my face wouldn't be in the picture. I had an ingrained sense of modesty, courtesy of thirteen years at all-girls Catholic schools. It had been a long time since anyone but my husband had seen my breasts, other than Dr. Diehl or my gynecologist—and those encounters didn't involve cameras. But I stood still, trying to suck it all in for the naked mug shots and thinking, *Suspects in a lineup get to keep their clothes on, at least.*

After the shoot, Dr. Rafizadeh asked me to stand in front of the exam table while he sat eye-level with my ladies and performed more than the routine breast exam. He lifted them up, pushed them together, measured them, and jotted notes as I stared at the ceiling wondering whether plastic surgeons ever considered having a wine fridge in their offices.

*If he was going to get this friendly, he could have offered me a glass of Chardonnay.*

As the exam came to an end, Dr. Rafizadeh asked, "So, what size do you want to be?"

I tried to ignore how self-conscious I was talking about boob size while standing there topless.

"Umm. Well, not too big. Maybe, a little smaller than I am now—

like a 36B," I said, pointing to my soft middle-aged 38C's and recalling a much younger me when my 36B's were the bomb.

"Really? Are you sure you don't want to go a little bigger? You want to be proportional to your body now."

*Gee, thanks.*

"I'm not sure I want to go much bigger . . ." my voice trailed off.

"Think about it. Either way, you are certainly going to be. . . um, perhaps a bit more pert."

My eyes met his when I finally stopped staring at the ceiling. The laughter I'd held back for most of this awkward encounter bubbled forth.

"Okay. And, more pert is good."

Dr. Rafizadeh smiled. His eyes sparkled and crinkled in the corners. At that moment he became *Dr. Sparkly Eyes* to me.

I scheduled my surgery for late August. In the meantime, my family was overdue for a trip to the beach.

# Chapter 12
## The Time in Between

To Do (6/23-7/6)
Cape Cod!
Go to Liam's for onion rings
Lose nails

I WOKE AT DAWN at my mother-in-law's beach house on Cape Cod in Harwich Port, Massachusetts—the Cape House, as I'd always called it. I reached for the soft blue cotton blanket at the foot of the wrought iron bed and pulled it close. Tim wasn't here yet to keep me warm, and the cool morning air was drifting off Nantucket Sound and across the sill of the window I opened the night before. As I breathed in, I noticed a funky odor. The scent reminded me of decaying fish mixed with a cloying sweetness.

"What is that smell?" I said to no one.

*The smell of decomposition. Of death.*

I sat up, groped for my eyeglasses on the bedside table, and switched on the light. I blinked against the bright glare and looked down at my hands. Overnight, liquid had pooled out along the side of my nails on my pinky, ring, and middle fingers. I raised them to my nose and sniffed.

Ugh. The odor was coming from my nails.

I pressed on my nails and even more liquid oozed out as my nails started to lift up from the nail bed.

*Sweet Jesus. Is this shit ever going to end?*

I pummeled my pillow.

*Cancer was taking over my entire body. Not just my breasts.*

Punch, punch.

*The Beast has already taken my hair. Soon it will get both boobs. Now it wants my nails, too. Really?*

I loved this place—it held our lives and each passage in them. So it was the perfect place for me to relax, to get some relief from the Beast. But no, it had followed me here, relentless.

*Dammit! How much more can I take? How much more does it want of me?*

I pulled my knees up to my chest, laid my head down, and rocked back and forth because I already knew the answer to that question. The Beast would take and take until there was nothing left.

I slammed the pillow against the bed as Ollie whimpered from his dog bed below.

⟞⟝

Unlike Tom and James, who were sleeping soundly downstairs, I wasn't going to get any more sleep. I got up, pulled on my exercise pants and tee shirt, and wrapped a Buff® around my head. I grabbed my sweatshirt from the peg on the back of the door. I crept downstairs with Ollie at my heel.

"Come on, buddy, let's go for a walk."

Ollie and I headed to the beach, letting the screen door close gently behind us so as not to wake the boys. We walked eastward along the shore.

Breathing in the cool, damp air, I started to calm down, paused, and offered a prayer of thanksgiving for this new day. I prayed for strength, healing, and the grace to keep going—one foot in front of the other—however broken I felt.

When I got back from my walk, I made coffee and settled into one of the chairs at the long cherrywood dining table where our family had shared countless meals. I was looking forward to some good ones when everyone arrived in a few days. For now, I was happy to savor my brew and enjoy the quiet morning, punctuated by the flutter and song of goldfinches breezing over the pool and alighting on the lavender plants in the garden.

⤳

The boys and I had arrived the day before. We planned to open the house and relax together before more of the family arrived, filling every bedroom. As I pulled into the driveway yesterday, and stepped out of the car, the crunch of the clamshells underfoot made a familiar and welcoming crackling sound. The soft, salt-scented air seemed to lower my heart rate, and I could feel my blood pressure go down the minute I filled my lungs.

I heard a screen door slam in the distance and panicked. I'd taken off my baseball cap during the five-hour drive from New Jersey. I reached in the car, grabbed my hat from the seat, and pulled it onto my bald head. I glanced across the street—there was no one in sight. I breathed a sigh of relief. I did not want to have a cancer conversation as soon as I arrived, savoring my small moment of privacy.

I usually took my time walking up the flagstone path to the Cape House—with its familiar weathered, gray cedar shingles and shiny black shutters and front door—and would run my fingers through the brilliant blue hydrangeas in the garden on my way. Instead, I breezed right up the steps, wanting to get inside and out of view. Pushing open the door on its squeaky hinges, walking into the rooms, which never changed with the passage of time, and closing the door behind me, I could feel the tension ease slightly from my neck and shoulders.

The white mantel, lined with old blue-green glass bottles, shells, and candles waiting to be lit, looked exactly as it had when we left last year. I cranked open all the windows in the kitchen and dining room to let in the summer breeze scented by the enormous lavender bush growing lush and full beneath them. I opened a pair of French doors facing the deck and pool beyond and stepped outside, breathing in my favorite fragrance—the sea, the beach grasses, and the flowers in the garden—grateful that I could.

With each trip to the car unloading our luggage and bags of food and supplies, I replayed years of memories in this special spot, like a slideshow in my mind. The first summer Tim and I stayed here in 1996, I was pregnant with Katie. I recalled other years where I'd walk with one crying baby or another to the local Dunkin' Donuts, only to find the snaking line of other bleary-eyed parents pushing strollers and waiting for coffee. I remembered marching the small army of kids and their stuff to the beach through the dunes or *tickle grass*, as Katie called it when she was a toddler.

Year after year, we'd gather for the Fourth of July. The Cape House became the place where the dozen Corrigan grandchildren bunked together, went to the beach, fought with each other, ate ice cream on hot summer nights, and grew like weeds. Like the kids, the parents and grandparents more or less did the same (fortified by many adult beverages and buttery seaside meals).

If I were gone, would they remember how much this place meant to me, how much I loved it?

I tried to push those thoughts from my mind, but it was hard. Tim's dad, Bob, gone three years then, loved the Cape House too. His presence lingered in photos, in his heavy yellow slicker hanging in the garage, in his bread-baking equipment and exotic condiments in the pantry, and in the errant golf club still propped in a corner next to the back door—he loved to practice chipping over the pool. Though the Beast claimed him in the end, I still saw Bob in Tim, his brothers, and the grandchildren. Tim often sat where his dad had and practiced chipping over the pool, and if Tim wasn't around, Tom, too, sat in Bob's favorite chair, next to the stack of old CDs—Bob's favorite jazz standards that no one wanted to listen to and that no one would dare get rid of.

*If I were gone, would they sit in my favorite rocker on the deck and remember me with a book in hand?*

When the boys and I finished unpacking, I picked up our favorite New England dinner—chowder, fish and chips for the boys, and a lobster roll for me. We enjoyed our first meal around the familiar table. The boys were looking forward to their cousins' arrival, and I was looking forward to a good night's sleep in my favorite place.

~

After I enjoyed my morning coffee, I checked the time. It was nearly nine o'clock; Dr. Abbasi's office would be open by now.

I called and spoke with one of the physician assistants about the disgusting state of my fingernails. She told me that nail damage or nail loss was yet another side effect, caused by the drugs' destruction of the cells in my nail beds. Worse, I was right about the smell: it *was* decaying flesh. I shivered when she said as much to me. The nurse suggested soaking my nails in warm water and tea tree oil.

Before I could dwell on my nails any longer, Tom and James wandered in, wiping sleep from their eyes, and sat at the table with me.

"Well good morning, you two. You must have been tired from the trip. I've been up for hours. It's nearly nine o'clock. Do you want breakfast?"

I made the boys breakfast and asked what they wanted to do for the day. They decided they would like to go down to Nauset Beach in Orleans. Although the day was overcast and cool, the boys wanted to swim in the ocean instead of Nantucket Sound. I wanted not to think about the fact that my nails were rotting off, so I was up for anything they wanted to do.

We found a spot by a sandbar and tide pool. The sound of the ocean's waves calmed and soothed my spirit, and I tried to stop obsessing over my nails. They'd grow back eventually, I supposed (*and they did—almost two years later*).

Tom and James walked along the misty shoreline, stopping every few feet to pick up a shell or some other treasure. Tom even took a swim, then fell shivering on the sand next to me.

At lunchtime, we crossed the lot to go to Liam's—the gray-shingled shack on Nauset Beach that served New England beach food—for fried fish sandwiches and the best onion rings on the Cape, maybe even the planet. They were thin, lightly battered, and not greasy.

As we waited for our orders, Tom asked, "Mom, do you think we can come back here again?"

"What do you mean, Tom? When your cousins come up in a few days?"

"No, I mean later in the summer. Do you think we can come back to the Cape?"

"Honestly, Tom, I don't know. It will depend on how I feel."

"Oh. Okay."

Tom looked away over the dune, toward the water. Though he wouldn't say so, I knew my cancer had hit him the hardest of my three children. He avoided me at home, often leaving the room when I walked in, and he didn't talk much with me. I knew it pained him to see me dealing with the same disease that had laid waste to his grandfather, whom Tom missed terribly.

"I'm sorry that I don't have an answer. If I can make it happen, I'll get you back up here later this summer, okay?"

Tom nodded and quickly brushed his hand across his eyes. At that moment, our order was called.

We chomped on our fried fish sandwiches and shared the perfect onion rings I'm sure weren't listed on any cancer prevention diet. I pulled them from their paper wrapper, one at a time, and popped them in my mouth, savoring the salty, sweet onions under the light, crunchy batter. I wasn't worried about fat and calories and licked every one of my fingers as I ate.

For all it had taken, the Beast had given me a few things, and this moment was one of them: an appreciation for simple pleasures. I reveled in this moment at a salt-and-wind-battered picnic table with my boys as waves crashed on the shore in the distance. Where else would I want to be, sick or healthy?

⌒

Liam's at Nauset Beach is gone now, victim to the vicious Nor'easters that pounded New England's coast the last few years. A small mercy, the onion rings survive at Liam's wife's joint in the town of Brewster. They remain one of my guilty pleasures.

⌒

Three days later, Jeanne, Tim, and three of his brothers and their families arrived. The Cape House overflowed with the fifteen of us and three dogs. The sounds of kids splashing in the pool, doing battle over who got the top bunk, and the grill sizzling with Italian sausage and burgers filled the air. While Tim and his brothers ribbed each other about their cooking skills, Jeanne and I sipped cranberry juice and tonics with lime as we sat in our favorite rockers on the deck.

At that moment, it didn't matter that my nails were falling off, that I was bald and had to wear a hat or a scarf so the kids wouldn't freak out, or that I was having surgery in a month. All the people, all the years and all the memories in that special house infused my heart with love.

Midway through our vacation, Tim and I woke to the sound of thunder and rain on the roof. Up until then, no rain had fallen.

I curled under his arm, welcoming a change in the weather and in our routine.

"I guess it's not a beach day," I said.

"I guess we'll have to stay here then," Tim grinned, pulling me toward him.

"Oh, Tim, I don't know," I hedged.

He held my face and began to kiss me. "You're beautiful," he whispered into my ear as he kissed my neck.

Slow warmth moved down my body to deep within my pelvis. Then, I pulled away.

"I'm not beautiful though. Not without any hair. And, I'll look even worse in another month when my breasts are gone."

I sat up, pulling my knees to my chest. Tim sat up too and looked into my eyes.

"Chris, you're everything to me. I love you, not your hair, not your breasts... *you*. *You* will always be beautiful to me."

He took my hands in his and held them close against his chest.

"I love you, too," I said.

Tim pulled me into his arms. We made love with a gentle easiness at first, then with an intensity and urgency to match the storm outside. Taking refuge in each other, we shuddered as the thunder boomed and cracked above us. We fell apart, panting, and drifted into sleep as the storm passed out to sea.

The early evening, when the sky turned a steely blue, was my favorite time on the Cape. In French, it was called *l'heure bleue* or the blue hour—the time in between, suspended between day and night, where earth and sky were equally luminous. During these deepening hours, our family sat on the deck eating stuffed quahogs and laughing at old jokes and stories.

Afterwards, I lit the candles on the mantel and table, savoring their soft glow as we gathered for dinner. Over this night's steamed lobster feast, Tom shared plenty of fish tales about the *huge* stripers he caught and released. We lingered at the table until James and Bella asked, "When are we going to get ice cream at Sundae School?"

"It's our last night. I'll go. Who else wants to come?" I said.

"I'll go," said Jeanne.

"Me too," said Tim.

"If any of you are not going, what do you want us to bring back?" I asked.

Tim's brothers shouted orders at us as the kids grabbed their flip-flops and sweatshirts. Then Jeanne, Tim, and I walked the few blocks to our favorite ice cream parlor with all eight of the cousins.

I found a spot at a picnic table nearby. I watched as parents and grandparents, children and grandchildren, different generations at each picnic table and bench, enjoyed the simplicity of ice cream on a July night. I glanced at our crew of kids sitting around the table next to me and saw them as they were in that moment—as teens and tweens—and all the years before—as children, toddlers, and babies in strollers.

Tim handed me an ice cream cone packed with my favorite flavor, sweet cream and walnuts. I only ate one ice cream cone a year, and this was the one. It was sweet, but not too sweet, and the walnuts provided a satisfying, yet slightly bitter crunch. Each bite encapsulated the tears and the love, the yin and yang, the time in between, of my days at the Cape House that summer.

# Chapter 13
## Not Yet

To Do (7/7-8/24)
Finish chemo
Have mastectomy

THE DAY AFTER I got home from the Cape, I returned to the infusion center for my final chemotherapy treatment and in a rush of happy impulsivity posted *Done!* on my Facebook wall. I wanted to feel the excitement of closing the chemotherapy chapter of the story, even though I had many more to go in my treatment plan: in three weeks I would return to the infusion center for the first of twelve Herceptin treatments. Although each treatment would only take about an hour (as opposed to the six or seven hours of chemotherapy) and Herceptin's side effects weren't as severe, I wouldn't be free of the infusion pump, the blood tests, and tri-weekly visits with Dr. Abbasi for eight more months.

I started taking Tamoxifen, the estrogen-suppressing drug used to prevent the recurrence of estrogen-positive breast cancer like mine, around the time my chemo ended. I would continue to experience side effects on this drug—dry skin, joint pain, thinning hair, loss of sexual libido—and I wasn't excited over the prospect of any of that. I also had to face my surgery in six weeks.

Truth was, I was far from being *done*, and my Facebook post was a false positive of sorts, but one I needed to see at that moment. The reality was that I'd reached the treatment *wall*, and I was physically, mentally, and emotionally exhausted. This reminded me of the twenty-mile mark a runner hits during a marathon. Based on what my running friends have told me, that's the moment when the runner feels completely depleted—and yet still has six miles to go to get to the end. To combat the discouragement and helplessness that accompanies the fatigue, veteran runners often will focus on the things they can control—like their form—so they'll run more efficiently and find a pace to finish the race.

While I've only run one half-marathon, I'll never forget the last three miles of that race. I thought it would never end. To keep going, I gave myself small goals: run to the next light pole, run to the next building, run to the next street light.

This was what I kept doing this summer. I couldn't eliminate my fatigue or the emotional strain—but I could try to keep myself moving forward.

⌒

The balance of the summer became a study in the art of distraction from my illness not only for me, but also for my family. Tom hiked and camped in the backcountry of New Mexico at Philmont Scout Reservation, a Boy Scout high adventure camp. I marveled at his strength and fortitude to hike eight to ten miles a day, especially since on some days, I couldn't summon the strength to make a cup of tea.

James enjoyed his days at a local camp. When James came home each afternoon, we often headed to the pool where I'd sit in the shade and James would spend the hours swimming with his friends and goofing around.

Katie worked two jobs as a lifeguard and swim instructor at a private club, then as a hostess at the club's restaurant in the evening. As for Tim, he put in long hours at work trying to clear his calendar in advance of my surgery—then spent long hours on the golf course trying not to think about it.

When I wasn't resting or going off with the kids, I distracted myself the best way I knew: through words—reading and writing. By then, I had struck up a lively correspondence with Tim's aunts, Peg and Barbara. I loved getting their letters and notes filled with their perfect script in which they shared little nuggets about their lives. Peg was in the middle of purchasing a new home and shared her decorating and remodeling schemes.

Barbara filled her letters to me with book recommendations, telling me about several authors whom I'd never read, including Gladys Taber who wrote *Stillmeadow Daybook,* a diary about the author's life on a farm, which Barbara suggested as a perfect book for recovering from surgery because I could dip into it, put it down, and return to it easily. While I wasn't sure that I'd like *Stillmeadow,* I ordered it and wrote back to Barbara, thanking her for the recommendations. She also made suggestions for trips to take once all the cancer business was behind me. While I was intrigued by the thought, I couldn't imagine planning any trips just then. I wanted the summer to end, and then I'd think about travel—*maybe.*

With four weeks left to go before my surgery, I went to a support group run by my surgeon's nurse, Karen. While I didn't go every month, when I did make it, I enjoyed talking with other women who were in it or who had gone through it. They got it.

At the end of that July meeting, Karen stopped me.

"Chris, would you mind putting together some thoughts or tips that I might share with other patients about going through chemo? It would be nice to have a patient's view."

Before I could think about what I was saying, I replied, "Sure, Karen, I'd be happy to do that for you."

On the ride home, I kicked myself.

*Why on earth did you say yes to Karen? You, my friend, really stepped in it this time. What could you possibly have to offer other patients?*

I pushed Karen's request from my mind and didn't return to it for months.

⌒

Two weeks out now, I made lists and scheduled appointments with a fury and urgency I hadn't experienced since I was about to give birth to James eleven years earlier.

| | |
|---|---|
| Dentist appointments. | Check |
| Haircuts for boys. | Check |
| Physical for James. | Check |
| School supplies. | Check |
| Back-to-school clothes. | Check |
| Update calendar with swim practices and cross-country meets. | Check |

My frenzied activity reminded me of the nesting I did in the days before I had the kids and wanted to make sure everything was ready: that there were enough diapers and wipes, that the sleepers were sorted and stacked on the changing table's shelves, and that the softest receiving blankets were folded over the crib rail. But this time, I wasn't nesting. I wasn't awaiting the birth of a child with all its attendant anticipation. I was catastrophe-planning for the worst outcome.

*What if I don't make it through the surgery?*

*Who would remember to do all of these things if I were gone?*

⌒

With just five days to mark off on my calendar, I met with Dr. Abbasi for my Herceptin appointment. He checked my labs and cleared me for surgery. Then, Dr. Abbasi told me that the surgical pathology would tell us whether the chemo worked.

"From your lips to God's ears," I replied, my voice shaky.

Dr. Abbasi paused with his forehead furrowed and said, "You have to stay positive. Just stay positive."

I nodded and, pushing down the lump down in my throat, asked, "Dr. Abbasi, would you please come see me after the surgery?"

"You know, Chris, it's not really necessary. The surgeons don't need help from the oncologists."

I wanted to cry. Dr. Abbasi helped me to keep going, to keep pushing through, and I couldn't bear that he would leave me alone when I was most frightened. If I ever needed his quiet, calm reassurance, it was then.

"It doesn't matter if the surgeons want you there. I'm asking. Would you please stop by and see me?" I said, sounding more like an adolescent than an adult as my voice rose in panic.

Sensing my distress, Dr. Abbasi stopped typing his notes on the computer, turned toward me, and in his peaceful manner, replied.

"Of course. I'll stop by next week after my rounds."

I exhaled a sigh of relief. "Thank you."

"Go, go," he said, shooing me out of his office. "It's time for your Herceptin. I'll see you next week."

When I got home from my appointment, a package from Barbara was waiting for me. She sent me *A Fine Romance: Falling in Love with the English Countryside* by Susan Branch. In her note she suggested we consider going to England the following year. I couldn't imagine any type of trip so I put *A Fine Romance* aside and turned to *Stillmeadow* that afternoon. Published in 1955, it chronicled a different time and place, as the author recorded her life in rural Connecticut. It was a sweet book, nostalgic, but not sappy. The book became a welcome distraction—the perfect book for recovering from anything.

⁓

On the day before the surgery, I turned my head away from the radiologist to stare at the ceiling, papered with a calming forest scene, and imagined being far away from the windowless radiology suite where I was undergoing sentinel node mapping. This procedure involved injecting my breasts with a radioactive fluid that burned with breath-taking intensity. This fiery fluid, I was told, would find its way to the sentinel lymph node, the one closest to the tumor, so Dr. Diehl would know what to biopsy the next day. The radiologist apologized with every injection and let me take a brief break to catch my breath. Through the worst of it the nurse held my hand.

After that less-than-pleasant experience, I returned to Dr. Rafizadeh to be marked before the surgery. Again I stood there topless, staring at the ceiling.

As Dr. Rafizadeh marked my breasts, neck, and chest with Sharpie markers, he asked, "Are you sure you don't want to go a little bigger? You know, to be proportional."

I forced myself to look right into Dr. Rafizadeh's sparkly eyes as I replied, "I don't think so."

I believe I heard him sigh.

I returned to counting the ceiling tiles, and he finished sketching on me.

That night, with only eight hours until Tim drove me to the hospital, I cried. I cried all of the tears I hadn't already shed.

*What if the chemo didn't work? What if we went through these last five months for nothing?*

"I've run out of brave," I said to Tim as he held me close.

"I know, love. I know," he said as he wiped my tears away once more. My sobs subsided, and I fell into a fitful sleep.

The following morning, a whirlwind of nurses and doctors

appeared in the small pre-operative cubicle where I was trembling under several heated blankets on a narrow stretcher. The doctors and nurses played the question game with me to ensure I was who I said I was and to confirm why I was there.

When it was time for the nurse to wheel me into the operating room, Dr. Diehl appeared by my side, his green-hazel eyes smiling down at me.

"Are you ready?"

I nodded. I couldn't speak, my voice lost to the fear gripping my throat.

Tim squeezed my hand, kissed me goodbye, and turned away. I was wheeled into the operating room. I prayed my last Hail Mary and pictured Tim, Katie, Tom, and James in my mind's eye before I fell into the dark.

I woke up in recovery to bright lights and the recovery room nurse trying to rouse me from the anesthesia. Her voice sounded closer than her body appeared to me in the glare of the cold, white lights. I felt the cold oxygen blowing in my face and tried to push it away, only to have my hand firmly pushed down.

I could hear the nurse urging me to sit up and breathe deeply. I blinked a few times and tried to focus on my chest. Solid mounds bumped through the hospital gown where my boobs once lived.

*HMMMM. They might be a little small after all . . .*

I sat up and breathed deeply at the nurse's urging to get my oxygen level up; I wouldn't be moved to my room until it was high and steady. The monitors beeped quietly to my side.

I pulled the blanket up to my neck. I was cold, and my throat was sore. The nurse brought me ice chips and apple juice to sip. As I drank the juice, I became less groggy. A short while later, Tim joined me.

"Hey, beautiful," he said and kissed my forehead.

"Not really, but you're sweet," I croaked, my throat sore and dry from the anesthesia.

I asked him what time it was; it was mid-afternoon. He fed me ice chips and as he did, I remembered that Mom had done the same for me all those years ago after my surgeries when I was a teen.

Tim told me the doctors said the surgery went well. I noticed his face looked tired and drawn.

"Tim, you need to go home and get some sleep. I'm going back to sleep as soon as they move me upstairs."

"I'll go as soon as they come to bring you up."

Before I could ask about the kids, Tim added, "The boys are fine. Katie worked all day, and one of your friends dropped off dinner for tonight," he said, with relief in his voice.

"I have good friends. We're lucky to have them." I smiled at Tim.

My girlfriends had set up a month-long meal train and driving schedule for James and Tom because it would be several weeks before I could drive. It comforted me to know that my friends and neighbors would take care of the feeding and people-moving for me.

Tim nodded and wiped his eyes. He took my hand.

"I love you," he said.

"Love you too. We made it, you know—this far, at least."

We sat in silence as a small measure of peace washed over me. The nurse came over and told us that it was time for me to move to my room. Tim went home so he could sleep.

I slept for ten hours until the following morning. As promised, Dr. Abbasi stopped by early to see me. He told me he had checked in with the nurses and checked on all my medications. All was as it should be. His presence calmed and reassured me, as it had for the last five months. He left, and I fell back to sleep.

Later that day, Dr. Diehl and Dr. Rafizadeh arrived to check my incisions and drains while I stared at the ceiling. Then I asked Dr. Diehl when he hoped he'd have the pathology report back.

"It's going to just be a few more days, Chris. I hope we'll have it by the end of the week."

"Why does everything take so long?" I groused.

"I know it's hard. I promise I'll call you as soon as we have it. The good news for today is, I think you'll be ready to go home tomorrow. But if you do want to go home tomorrow," Dr. Rafizadeh added as he replaced the dressings, "you need to get up and get moving, so you can get back to living your life."

"Well, okay, then, I guess I'm getting up," I replied.

Taking Dr. Rafizadeh's words to heart, and after the doctors left, I started walking up and down the long hospital hallway. I wasn't as sore as I thought I would be. I walked almost two miles that first day back and forth down the beige corridor, passing the coffee and snack station (a nice treat), the nurses' station, and dark wooden doors every few feet. My decision months earlier to walk every day and to lift weights twice a week through treatment had paid off.

After my walk, I was ready to climb back into bed.

⌒

As the doctors, my family, and friends visited, I remembered the days during the last week of August 1981 after I had surgery to remove my spleen before I started radiation therapy.

My recovery in the hospital took at least a week. Trina visited daily. The principal of our high school and my fearsome math teacher also visited me. I never expected that those two would visit me, especially not Sister Marie! They gave me a stuffed koala bear, our school's mascot, that I kept on my bed during the long months to come. They assured me they would pray for me every day.

One of my dad's colleagues also visited me a few times. He brought me books and told me all about a wilderness survival program called Outward Bound. He was hoping to convince my mom and dad to let me go the following summer. I didn't think they'd go for that, but I liked listening to his stories about camping, rock-climbing, and hiking. A day or two before I was discharged, he stopped by and gave me a book called *To Know by Experience*, about an Outward Bound program in North Carolina.

In the book, he wrote me a note and told me I would overcome the challenge I faced with *good humor, fortitude and determination.* I didn't share his optimism, although I read the book over and over. I drew some comfort from the photographs of the young people on their hikes and rafting trips and their journal entries about what they learned from their experiences in the wilderness.

After I finished radiation therapy, I never reopened that book or went on an Outward Bound experience. It remained shut for decades, like that chapter in my life of my first cancer, and the memory of the book faded from my mind.

⌒

After all of the visits and walking up and down the hospital hallway, I fell into a sound sleep. I was going home in the morning to the place where I most wanted to be.

⌒

# The Practical Reality
**Clothing Recommendation**

One great piece of advice I received was to buy a couple of pairs of button-front pajamas and shirts before my surgery because I was unable (and not allowed) to lift my arms higher than my shoulders. I found a couple of brightly colored and patterned ones at the local mall, and they helped lift my spirits as I recovered.

This style also makes it easier to get to the drains when they need to be emptied. You can unbutton the pajamas or shirt and slip out, rather than try hold a tee shirt up under your neck with your chin like a contortionist (speaking from experience, there!).

**Drain Pouches**

When I had my breast surgery, one great piece of advice I received was to buy a comfortable surgical bra with pouches for the drains. The pouches attach to the bra, and relieve the tugging or pulling sensation of the drainage tubes while they are in the incision.

## Drawing Strength From Other Generations

When I was in treatment, I leaned on my husband's aunts, Barbara and, especially, Peggy. We wrote, texted, and talked. Peggy had non-Hodgkin's lymphoma thirty years before my breast cancer diagnosis and related to what I was going through; sure enough, her notes and letters struck the right note each time. I always smiled when I found a letter waiting for me when I got home from my appointments because in them, Peggy reminded me again and again that I would get through it—one step, one day, one week, one month, one year at a time. Even today, I still enjoy Peg's letters, her perspective and the place of peace she's found for herself.

One of my friends who went through treatment for lymphoma at the same time I was in treatment for breast cancer struck up friendships with many of the patients she met, some much older than she. She enjoyed how they sometimes traveled in pairs, filled out their forms aloud, and talked on their flip phones so all the world could hear. And, they did not care. She found them to be prepared, carefree, unrushed, and supported in the waiting room, and that made her smile. By finding joy in her observations, she was able to let go of her anxiety about her own appointments.

## Lymphedema

While I didn't experience lymphedema personally, many breast cancer survivors have told me that they wished they'd learned more about lymphedema, an abnormal swelling that can develop as a result of an accumulation of lymph in an area of the body, such as the arm, hand, breast, or torso. While I'm sure my doctors talked to me about this side effect to my breast surgery, I can't say I remember much about such a conversation, as I was drowning in the tidal wave of other information about my treatment.

The Lymphatic Education and Research Network (lymphaticnetwork.org) reports that the risk for getting lymphedema is most closely related to lymph node removal. In addition, patients who undergo radiation therapy also are at heightened risk for lymphedema.

According to Breastcancer.org, lymphedema usually develops gradually. Symptoms may include intermittent tingling or numbness, achiness, feelings of fullness or heaviness, puffiness or swelling, and decreased flexibility or tightness in the hand, arm, chest, breast, or underarm areas. Early treatment of lymphedema is important, so tell your doctor if you experience any of these symptoms.

If you have questions about lymphedema, talk to your doctor to understand its symptoms and treatment.

**Recliners**

My breast surgeon and plastic surgeon didn't want me to sleep lying on my back for a few weeks after surgery and suggested that I sleep in a recliner. We don't own a reclining chair (and didn't know anyone who did), so I slept propped up on pillows. It wasn't terribly comfortable.

Whether you love them or hate them as furniture, a reclining chair is a nice thing to lay your hands on when recovering from breast surgery. I'm not suggesting you go out and buy one, but borrow one if you can. Friends of mine who used recliners after their surgery were glad they did.

**Wedge Pillow Hack**

If you don't have a recliner and can't borrow one, a wedge pillow is the next best thing. It keeps the upper body elevated enough for recovery but is comfortable so you can sleep. I wish I'd known about wedge pillows when I was recovering from surgery.

They are available online, and at most department stores and home goods retailers.

# Chapter 14
## Answered Prayers

To Do (8/25-9/16)
Laugh at pink flamingos
Wait for surgical pathology report
Learn to get dressed in the dark
Say thank you

AFTER MY DISCHARGE FROM the hospital the following morning, Tim and Jenny brought me home. They eased me into the car and inserted comfort pillows between the seatbelt and my chest to protect the incisions. I leaned against the leather seat, closed my eyes, and exhaled a sigh of gratitude to be going home.

As we drove up our street, I glanced out the car window. Someone had covered our front lawn with about fifty plastic pink flamingos.

"Tim, what's with the birds?"

"Katie will explain it to you. I think it was one of her swim team friends."

"Too funny," I laughed.

In the kitchen, Katie, Tom, and James were waiting. Tim reminded them not to squeeze too hard as each one gave me a gentle hug. I asked Katie about the flamingos, and she handed me a card from another swim family explaining that we'd been *flocked* and wishing me a smooth recovery.

Our friends, Elizabeth and Mark, sent a bouquet of white hydrangeas and pink roses with a note. *Stay strong and embrace the love. You have a great team of supporters, and we will continue to lift you up in the coming weeks,* it said.

A big package also was waiting for me from one of Tim's colleagues. In it was a soft, gray and white blanket that Tim tucked in around me once he helped me get settled in the rich brown-colored suede club chair in the family room next to the window. I fell asleep until dinner, and afterward, I went up to bed. I didn't mind sleeping sitting up too terribly much though. I was simply happy to be in my own bed.

The next morning as I was sitting in the family room, my cell phone rang. I saw Dr. Diehl's number flash on the screen and my spine stiffened. Terror's icy tentacles again seized my stomach and squeezed it tight. A cold sense of dread spread through my pelvis and down my legs.

*Oh God, oh God.*

*What if the chemo didn't work?*

*What if we went through the past five months for nothing?*

*What will happen now?*

*What if the cancer was in my nodes or has even spread?*

*More chemo?*

*Radiation?*

*Please don't let me die. Not now. Not after all of this.*

*What will happen to Tim and the kids?*

*Please, Lord. Please.*

The phone rang again. I had to answer it. I pushed those thoughts away. I tapped my phone and answered.

"Hi, Dr. Diehl."

"Hello, Chris," he replied, pausing for a moment.

I couldn't tell from the tone of Dr. Diehl's voice whether he was about to give me good news or bad news.

He went on. "I have great news for you. We have excellent results from pathology. The tumor is gone, your margins are clear, and your nodes are clear. The chemo worked."

Dr. Diehl sounded so pleased! I imagined him with a smile on his face.

"Oh, thank God!" I exclaimed.

Relief flooded through every cell of my body, and the icy tentacles grasping my insides melted away. I relaxed my spine and sighed as my heartbeat slowed. I exhaled slowly and prayed.

*Thank you. Oh God, thank you.*

I noticed Tim standing next to me, mouthing, "What, what?"

I gave him the thumbs-up sign and watched his face break into an ear-to-ear smile.

"See, Dr. Diehl, you finally got to give me some good news after all these months. Can you send the report to Dr. Abbasi?"

"I'm sending it to him now. How are you feeling otherwise? Not too sore, I hope."

"I feel fantastic now," I laughed. "And the soreness is starting to subside."

"I'll see you in a couple of weeks, Chris."

"Thank you again for all of it, Dr. Diehl."

I ended the call and pulled Tim toward me. I wrapped my arms around his neck.

"It's gone. Thank God."

Tim started crying in joy, in relief, knowing the chemotherapy worked.

"We have to tell the kids," I said as my sister walked in from the patio where she had stolen a smoke.

"Tell them what, Chris?"

"Jenny, my surgeon called. My pathology is clean."

She gave me a kiss on the top of my porcupine head and rested her forehead against mine.

Tim called to the kids, who traipsed into the room looking puzzled. They gathered around me on the adjacent chair, ottoman, and sofa.

"The cancer's gone. The chemo worked. My doctor just called to tell me," I reported.

James gently hugged me, and I ran my fingers through his hair.

"That's the best news, Mom," Katie said as I reached over, took her hand, and squeezed it.

"Yeah, that's great, Mom. Does that mean your hair's gonna grow back now?" Tom asked, smiling at me.

I laughed and said, "It'll grow back in a few months. Listen to me, the three of you. You were so very brave. I know how hard it was for the past five months . . ."

My voice broke. I paused for a moment to collect myself and wiped my eyes.

"I'm incredibly proud of you, for your courage, for your strength. And, I love you all so much."

"We love you too, Mom," Katie said.

"Yeah, Mom," Tom added as he nodded his head.

For a while we sat together in silence. A weight had lifted off our family.

After a bit, the kids stood, one by one. Katie had to go to work. Tim offered to take the boys to the pool and told me I needed a nap. I didn't disagree. I was starting to flag. Before I could fall asleep though, I needed to tell the whole damn world this news.

First, I called my friend Athena. "It's gone. The pathology was clean."

"Oh, girlfriend," she replied, and then asked for all of the medical details—as she always did. I filled her in as best I could and told her I'd send her the report if she wanted to read it.

"No, you don't have to do that. But I am so happy for you."

"Thank you. I'm over the moon! It's feels like the weight of a thousand elephants is off my shoulders."

"We have to celebrate," Athena said.

"We do, but not yet. I still have the implant surgery and six more months of Herceptin. We'll celebrate when I'm done in March."

"Well, we'll go out for dumplings in a few weeks, then."

"I'd love that, Athena. You're the best."

After my call with Athena, I called or texted almost everyone else I knew: family, friends, anyone who had been with me along the way. Then, I followed Tim's advice and took a nap, exhausted from the emotion of it all.

As I drifted off to sleep, my mind returned to another conversation with a doctor and my parents, decades earlier.

⌣

Radiation therapy ended in early November 1981, and so in early December I went in for a follow-up appointment. At the visit, Dr. Charles told my parents and me that I didn't need any more treatment.

I watched as the smile spread across his face. It was the first time I had seen Dr. Charles smile.

A look of relief washed over my parents' faces. Mom pulled me close to her, placed her hand on my cheek, and whispered.

"Thank God."

My dad stood and shook Dr. Charles's hand, pumping it up and down.

I was so happy we wouldn't have to drive to Memorial Sloan Kettering every day, although Dr. Charles told us I would have to come back for periodic check-ups.

Dr. Charles told me I could get back to school and all my activities as soon as I felt up to it. I assured him I already did.

I was ready to have my life back, my normal, fifteen-year-old life.

⁓

After speaking with Athena and other friends and family, I slept for most of that day and the days to come. The surgery had knocked me out. Although I couldn't move around much, I felt calmer knowing that the chemotherapy did its job. I could hardly wait to recover from the surgery and start *living my life* again, as Dr. Rafizadeh said in the hospital. It would take time, but each day that passed was one step toward that goal.

As I recovered, Tim and Jenny hovered over me like two mother hens.

On the Sunday morning before my sister went home, Jenny announced it was time to get me *cleaned up*. She helped me wash my hair. She took off the itchy hospital surgical bra, removed the dressings, and cleaned all the orange Betadine from me. As she did that, I looked in the mirror for the first time at me, Version 1.5, with nary a nipple or areola in sight.

"Christ, Jen. I look like a Barbie doll with scars," I said, brushing at my eyes as they filled with tears.

"Sweetie. You won't be like this forever. You'll have the final implant and nipple reconstruction surgery in a few months," she reminded me.

"I know, but look at this . . ." I said, gesturing to my chest. "I don't look like a woman anymore."

I choked on my tears, horrified that the breasts that my husband and I loved, and with which I had nursed and loved my children, were gone and replaced by round, rigid expanders used to create a pocket under the chest muscle where implants would be inserted months later.

I wasn't prepared for this emotional reaction to the physical loss of my breasts; it was a shock to my deepest sense of myself. I had a hard time reconciling my happiness about chemotherapy and my sadness over the physical reality of the loss of my breasts.

Jenny wrapped my robe around me and let me cry on her shoulder, rubbing my back the way our mom would have done.

"Give it time, Chris. You're going to get through the rest of this."

"Let's get me dressed, okay? I don't want to look anymore right now."

Jenny put clean dressings over my incisions and got me into my new surgical bra. She put the drains in their little pouches and attached them to the bra. Then she helped me get dressed. When the job was done, Jenny went home.

I tried not to think about any of it—how awful I looked to myself; how miserable I felt about my body; what I had lost.

⌒

Not thinking about my changed body and appearance was a big ask. So I fell back on my first and best line of defense: avoiding the awful.

In the months between my mastectomy and final implant surgery, I came up with new ways to avoid looking at myself. I wrapped myself in a towel before I looked in the mirror or put on a robe as soon as I stepped out of the shower. I figured out how to get dressed without looking down or, even better, got dressed in my darkened closet. I wouldn't show Tim what I looked like during those days immediately following the mastectomy. I knew he would say I remained beautiful to him or that he didn't care what I looked like as long as I was alive. But *I* cared.

Even though I knew I was more than my breasts, more than my appearance, and that our relationship was strong, I didn't feel whole. I felt like a broken teacup, one that had cracked and been glued together. While it could still hold tea, it didn't look or feel the same.

More than the feelings of brokenness, I also was afraid: *what if Tim looks at me and turns away in horror or disgust? Or worse, what if he gives me a pity-stare?*

I knew that he would do none of those things, and he didn't once I started getting dressed in front of him again after I became comfortable with my reconstructed body some months later. But during those early days, I couldn't bear the thought of the possibility. So, I put those thoughts in the Box and got dressed when Tim wasn't around.

⌒

After Jenny left, the final days of August seemed to melt together. Normally, we would have spent those days at the beach, but Labor Day came and went with us still at home and me recovering.

School started up again for the boys, and Katie returned to college. A week later, I saw Dr. Rafizadeh, who removed the surgical drains and told me that I could finally shower instead of taking sponge baths, drive locally, and walk. But I still wasn't to do any heavy lifting or go to the gym yet.

I could live with these baby steps, and I made a mental note to call Athena and schedule time to walk with her again.

Dr. Rafizadeh said he would see me in six weeks and decide on a date for the final implant surgery.

I also had my last visit with Dr. Diehl. He checked the incisions, said I looked great, and that he would see me in a year. I left his office a little sad, knowing that I wouldn't see him, his kind smile, and his green eyes for twelve months.

⌒

A few days later, I saw Dr. Abbasi for my first Herceptin treatment since the surgery. When I walked into his office, he smiled and pulled me into a gentle hug. He asked me how I felt, and I assured him I wasn't sore, and healing well.

"Do you know when your final surgery will be yet?"

"Not yet. I'll see Dr. Rafizadeh in a little over a month. He said it could be three or four months," I sighed.

"It will get here before you know it."

"I hope so. I'm so ready for this to be over."

"I know, Chris. Let's take a look at the pathology report."

He sat at his computer and reviewed the surgical pathology report with me. He noted that the tumor was gone—or as he said, *melted away*, as he hoped it would all those months ago.

"You were right. The chemo worked," I said.

"Of course, it worked. That combination of drugs always works so well. It wasn't me. It was God's will."

*Insha Allah. And Amen.*

It was time for me to thank Dr. Abbasi. I owed him that.

Before I thanked him though, I thought back to when I thanked Dr. Forte so many years ago, when I was a different person: a young woman, less experienced with life as well as with cancer.

⌒

After my radiation therapy ended, Dr. Forte and I kept in touch. Right when I was about to graduate from college, I showed up for my annual visit at age twenty-one.

Dr. Forte looked up from his cluttered desk, piled high with medical journals and charts, and smiled.

"Hi, kiddo."

Dr. Forte had never stopped calling me that, even over the many years.

I sat in one of the chairs facing his desk and noted the ever-present cigar smoldering in the ashtray.

"You know, those things can give you cancer. You should quit," I said.

I badgered Dr. Forte about his habit at every visit.

"So, you're the doctor now." He glanced at me over the top of his wire-rimmed glasses, his dark eyes dancing.

"Nope, going to law school," I retorted, smiling back at him.

"We all have our ways of getting through, kiddo. You have to learn not to judge. We're done now. It's been almost seven years. I don't need to see you anymore. So, get out of my office and go live your life. Marry a nice Italian boy."

I was stunned. I wasn't prepared to hear those words, although I understood them. He had other patients, and I had long stopped treatment. I was *cured*, as the doctors at Memorial Sloan Kettering told me. But how would I be okay if Dr. Forte wasn't watching over me and checking on me, even if only once a year? I started to cry.

Dr. Forte pulled a handkerchief out of the inner pocket of his suit jacket and passed it to me. I wiped my tears away.

"Thanks for all you've done for me, Dr. Forte. I won't ever forget any of it."

I stood up, and Dr. Forte rose from his desk chair. He wrapped me in one of his tremendous bear hugs, the scent of his cigar lingering in the wool of his suit. When he let go, I smiled up at him, then turned to leave.

"One more thing, kiddo." His tone shifted to his serious doctor voice. I turned back, and Dr. Forte looked straight into my eyes.

"Don't forget to have annual mammograms. Start them early, in your thirties, okay?"

"I will, Dr. Forte," I replied, not knowing why he was telling me this at twenty-one, and not prescient enough to ask.

I filed his words away. I knew I would deal with it in ten years or so, but it was the last thing I wanted to think about then.

⌒

Thirty-five years later, I finally understood Dr. Forte helped save my life not once, but twice, with his care and advice.

And like that conversation with Dr. Forte all those years before, I wasn't sure how I'd keep it together as I spoke to Dr. Abbasi.

"Dr. Abbasi, I want to thank you. Through all of this, you've been calm and confident about the treatment. Even on those days when I had enough and was trying to get out of the boat, so to speak, you kept me in there and steered me forward."

My throat closed around the words.

"I'm sorry, I'm a little emotional." I admitted.

"Of course, you're emotional, Chris. You had it harder than most patients. Most patients have never had cancer. They come in here, and they don't know what to expect. You went through it once, and you had to relive all of those memories from then. You were only, what, fifteen? It was a traumatic experience for you, like PTSD."

I was shocked to hear the insight. Dr. Abbasi saw the ghosts of cancer past following me around throughout my treatment, though I'd never spoken of them. I imagine that's why he handled me so deftly, particularly during those times when I was acting like a teenager.

"You have a hard job," I said, trying to change the subject.

"No. This is why I do this. The great results make it all worthwhile. I tell my staff, the medical students, and residents that they have to make an emotional connection with their patients. That's the most important thing."

Dr. Abbasi smiled his brightest smile, his eyes radiating light and warmth. We sat in silence for a moment. Dr. Abbasi and I had made a connection, one that would last another lifetime.

"Now go, go. It's time for your Herceptin," he said as he ushered me out of his office. But as I walked toward the infusion room, Dr. Abbasi called to me. I looked over my shoulder at him, his espresso-colored eyes smiling.

"One more thing, Chris. The next time you see Dr. Rafizadeh, tell him I said, 'I did my job, now you finish yours.'"

I laughed. "You could text him or tell him yourself, you know. You docs see each other all the time."

"No, it's better if he hears it from you. I'll see you in three weeks."

I settled myself in the infusion center feeling lighter in mind and spirit that day than I'd felt in months.

# Chapter 15
## Beginning

To Do (10/16 to 12/16)
Search for *normal* again
Write list for Karen
Plan for Thanksgiving
Stevie Nicks!

THE WEEKS PASSED, AND by October, I began to feel more myself. The soreness in my chest disappeared. The incisions healed. The fog lifted from my brain. My hair started to grow back, and I began cooking again.

I filled my calendar with PTO meetings, swim team meetings and meets, and cross-country practices and meets. I'd begun to get my life back, although I still couldn't do some things, like lift anything heavier than a gallon of milk. So, one of my friends took me shopping every week, then unpacked my groceries at home. I really had the best friends.

⌣

I no longer need anyone to take me grocery shopping, but when I push that grocery cart up and down the aisles today, I try to remember those moments when I couldn't, and say a little prayer of thanks because now I can.

⌣

On a crisp, morning, I went for my walk with Ollie because I still couldn't go to the gym. I walked down our quiet street, breathed in the cool air, and saw the dew-covered grass shimmer in the sunlight. As I turned the corner, I looked up at a perfect maple tree with its leaves turning. At that moment, the sunlight blazed through the tree, setting the orange-red leaves aglow. My breath caught in my throat, and I raised my eyes to the perfect autumnal blue sky.

*Thank you, thank you for getting me here. Thank you for now.*

When I got home from that walk, I knew I had to turn to Karen's request from earlier that summer for helpful tips or thoughts for other breast cancer patients. I'd never ignored a request for help this long; I had to write something for Karen.

*Where will I start? And, what will I say?*

I sat down at my desk and decided I would write Karen a list, a simple list, of the things that I knew then that I didn't know when I started down the breast cancer highway. It shouldn't take *that* long. How hard would it be to write a simple list?

*Pretty hard, apparently.*

⌣

On my follow-up visit later that week with Dr. Rafizadeh, we discussed my breast implant and nipple reconstruction surgery. As I walked into the exam room, I pulled my sweater off, my earlier unease about standing topless now gone. This time, instead of staring at the ceiling, I turned to Dr. Rafizadeh and pointed to the girls.

"You know, I think we need to go a little bigger. What do you think?

He smiled. "You have a little room. We can go a bit bigger."

Dr. Rafizadeh knew exactly what I needed, but I had needed time to figure it out myself. I understood now that all his subtle references to *proportion* were his polite way of saying, *Lady, you no longer have the body for 36Bs.*

I didn't, and I was okay with that.

He scheduled the surgery for late November.

With the surgery scheduled, I continued to write that list for Karen. Day after day, I'd sit at my desk and add to the list more of what I learned about having breast cancer. I wrote about the fear and uncertainty during those early days following my diagnosis. I wrote about my family, friends, and me, my faith, and my doctors. I wrote about how I got through chemotherapy and breast surgery. I didn't know as I was sitting at my desk then I was beginning to create a new life for myself as a writer, not of legal blogs and newsletters, but of subjects that mattered to me and that I hoped someday would help others.

My family didn't share my newfound enthusiasm. Once, when I brought up my writing over dinner when we recounted our days, Tom vented,

"Can you not, Mom? Your chemo is over. Surgery is over. Your hair is growing back. No one wants to hear about dumb, stupid breast cancer anymore. No one would want to read about it either."

"This is important to your mom, so try to be a little more supportive," Tim answered.

"I get what you're saying," I countered. "If it's making you upset or uncomfortable, I'll keep the talk to a minimum. But I do think this will help other people, sweetie."

"Oh, okay," Tom replied, rolling his eyes at me, "but it's still really annoying."

Notwithstanding that my family didn't engage in much cheerleading, I kept at it and put the finishing touches on my list for

Karen. When it was all said and done, it was more than a list, but rather, ten short essays about a particular thing I learned—from the emotional, to the spiritual, to the practical. I called it *What I Know Now.*

I emailed it to Karen, waited, and wondered whether she'd like it. I'd never written anything like this. It wasn't a legal brief or an article about an employment discrimination case. A few days later, she called me.

"Chris, I finished reading *What I Know Now.* I loved it, even though it's not really a list."

"Karen, you made my day. I know it's not the short, simple list you asked for, but when I started writing, I couldn't stop. I hope you can still use it though, for your other patients."

"Absolutely. I have one or two in mind already. Do you mind if I send it to them?"

"Not at all. That's why I wrote it."

"I want to share it with Dr. Diehl too, if that's okay. This is such a wonderful gift, Chris. I can't wait to share it. You also should give it to Dr. Abbasi. I think he'd love it."

"I'll think on that," I promised, "and thanks again for your kind words. They mean the world. I'll talk to you soon."

I hung up the phone, jumped out of my desk chair and danced around the kitchen to the music playing in my head.

*A gift*, no one had ever told me that my writing was a gift; it'd been called *well-reasoned, strongly argued*, and *precise*—but never a gift.

As I left the house to pick up James and Tom, I turned Karen's words over in my mind. I remembered the only other time I'd written about cancer: when I wrote about having Hodgkin's in early 1982, a few months after I'd finished radiation therapy and returned to high school.

One day I asked my forensics coach if I could write a speech about being a Hodgkin's patient based on my journal. She agreed.

I spent weeks writing and rewriting it on legal paper in ballpoint blue ink, then typed the speech on thin onionskin paper.

I wrote about the waiting room where I was the youngest patient.

I wrote about being alone with the Zapper.

I wrote about missing school, losing clumps of my hair, and throwing up every day on the ride home.

I wrote about how lonely the experience was and how my friend phoned me every night to help me make up a semester's worth of work.

I practiced the speech every day after school until I could give it with emotion, but without tears.

When I was ready, my coach entered me into the original oratory category at an invitational speech tournament at a high school in New York City. In the preliminary rounds, each student competed three times before three different judges. The speeches were scored according to various criteria, and the top eight students advanced to finals.

In my first round, my judge was the head speech coach of a rival high school. I stood before him in a navy blue suit, cream blouse, and navy heels, and began.

I watched his face remain expressionless above his dark suit and Roman collar. He wrote little on his scoring sheet. When I concluded, he told me that he was sorry I had to go through what I did. He said it must have been hard for me to write about the experience. He wished me well.

I left the small classroom for my next round puzzled by his reaction. I walked down the terrazzo hallway, passing statues of the Blessed Mother and other saints and paintings of former headmasters looking down at me, trying to make sense of his words. I didn't write the speech for sympathy; I wrote it to tell the story. I wanted him to listen and appreciate that.

After two more rounds, I learned I didn't final—but I wasn't surprised since it was the first time I had competed in original oratory.

When I arrived at practice on Monday afternoon after the tournament, my coach reviewed my score sheets with me as she always did. The judges declined to score the substance of the speech, finding it too hard, too personal and too emotional. It wasn't fair to judge the content, they said, although my presentation was excellent.

"But why isn't it fair, Sister? I've heard plenty of other students give original speeches about difficult topics: the Holocaust, the loss of a grandparent, the death of their dog. Why is my speech so different?"

My question hung in the air between us.

She paused before she answered.

"I think it would be best if you wrote another speech if you want to keep doing original oratory."

"That's not right. I worked hard on that speech."

"Christine," Sister replied, with an air of exasperation, "many of the judges are parents of children your age. They don't want to hear a speech about all that unpleasantness. It's upsetting to them. Don't you understand?"

"No, I don't. I don't at all," I said, not comprehending why it was up to me to make sure that the adults who were listening didn't get upset.

"Why not write a speech about ambition?" my coach asked.

"Ambition?" I replied.

"Yes, I have a poem about ambition. I've always wanted one of you girls to write about this."

My coach rustled around her steel desk until she found the ambition poem and handed it to me. I read the verses. I didn't want to write a speech about ambition.

"But Sister . . ."

"You're not giving that other speech again. I'm sorry."

"Not as much as I am."

I stormed out of her classroom with the ambition poem clenched in my hand.

I took my speech home and stuck it in my desk drawer along with my journal. I wrote another speech, this one about ambition, and I loathed it (I never won with it, either). By the end of my sophomore year, I stopped competing in original oratory and eventually threw my Hodgkin's speech and the journal away.

⌒

I'm not sure why I tossed my speech and journal—maybe in a bit of pique over the story's rejection. Or I may have cleaned out my desk before I went to college and couldn't imagine that I'd ever want to read my old journal and speech again. Whatever the reason, I wish I hadn't. I would have liked to reread my younger self's words, rather than rely on my memory of them.

Worse, in the bitter irony of memory, I can recite the opening lines of the ambition speech I hated to this day, but I cannot remember any of the words of my Hodgkin's speech.

I have heard it said that we remember only that which is memorable or that to which we attach a strong emotion. Perhaps that's true. I can recall that which I despised, but only the loss of the story I wanted to share remains.

⌒

By the time my next Herceptin infusion rolled around, I'd decided to give Dr. Abbasi a copy of my list, *What I Know Now*.

Why not? He went through it with me after all.

⌒

Thanksgiving approached. We would be hosting the whole family, and I was looking forward to the day to celebrate together. Jeanne came to stay with us for a few days to help with the preparations. We hadn't seen her since the end of the summer when she moved from her home, a stately Connecticut colonial, to an assisted living facility.

After Jeanne's husband died, she had a harder time managing her house and living on her own, then her own health declined, making the move inevitable. Tim and I had hoped, by having Jeanne help with the cooking and make her legendary lemon meringue pie, she wouldn't be upset over not having Thanksgiving at her home, as we had for years.

On the Wednesday before Thanksgiving, our kitchen hummed with activity. Tim chopped onions and celery, and I sautéed the sausage and sage for the stuffing my dad taught me to make. My thoughts always turned to my parents on Thanksgiving as I made their recipes—not only the stuffing, but also my mom's cranberry relish and the pies. I missed them as I cooked and thought about how much of our lives they'd never known, both having died so young. None of the kids ever knew my dad, though Katie had his artistic talent and Tom, his ability to tell a good tale. Only Katie has fleeting, vague memories of my mom (Katie was five when she died), but Katie can sing as beautifully as she did.

Jeanne joined us late in the morning. I'd laid out everything for her to make her flaky, buttery piecrust, as Jeanne never needed to follow a recipe. She looked at every ingredient placed out on the counter, bewildered and unsure where to begin.

Alzheimer's had stolen the pastry recipe Jeanne had learned during the family's days in France a lifetime ago. This memory, like many others, was gone—erased. I looked at Jeanne's face and wanted to cry and rage against the unfairness of all of it. In the span of three short years, Jeanne lost her beloved husband of forty-nine years, Tim and his brothers lost their dad, the kids lost their grandfather, I lost my breasts to cancer—and now Jeanne was losing her beautiful mind.

Life could be cruel and unforgiving at any age. We were powerless to stop or prevent any of it. I wanted to lie on the floor and kick my feet in a full-blown tantrum or lie in abject silence, demanding, like Job, that God explain this to me. I knew that didn't end well for Job, as God got the last word: *He who argues with God, let him answer it.* I also knew that none of it would get the pie in the oven.

"Hey, Jeanne. Do you want Katie to help you with the pie?" I asked.

"Yes, that would be grand," she said, clapping her hands. "Katie loves my lemon meringue pie."

Katie sat with Jeanne at the counter and made the pastry. I made the tart, smooth lemon curd. Jeanne whipped the egg whites and sugar into fluffy mounds and spread the meringue on parchment paper. Into the oven it went perfectly formed; out it came perfectly flat and stuck to the parchment. We had forgotten to add the cream of tartar to the meringue mixture or butter the parchment.

We managed to persuade the parchment to part company with the fallen meringue and placed it on top of the lemon curd-filled pastry. I looked at the less-than-perfect pie. It was a fitting metaphor for the year: one of tartness and sweetness, none of which was pretty.

On Thanksgiving morning, the turkey went into the oven. In a few hours, the kitchen smelled like sage and heaven. Tim's brothers arrived with their families; soon, our home was overflowing with aunts, uncles, cousins, dogs, and laughter.

I set the table with the rich burgundy cloth with the tree of life embroidered in gold thread in its center. As I ran my hand along the edge of the table to smooth the cloth, I offered my own silent prayer of thanksgiving that I was alive to share this day.

I placed the white Wedgewood china Tim and I had received as wedding gifts on the cloth, then I added the Waterford goblets that Jeanne had bought in Ireland decades earlier as a gift for her mother-in-law, and who had given them to us when we got engaged.

I placed my grandmother's sparkling silver serving pieces on the table. I glanced at the sideboard groaning with the pies resting on silver and crystal stands, some of which belonged to my dad's sisters.

So many generations had shared meals using these same beautiful objects. I could almost feel their presence: my family, Tim's family, our family together.

These heirlooms carried our collective family history and memories with them. When I picked up the Waterford, I didn't see a glass, I saw Helen, Tim's grandmother, sipping from that same glass and chatting about a recent movie or an interesting current event while holding a cigarette, smudged with her red lipstick, between her fingers.

I saw my maternal grandmother's face in the shimmering silver. She was born in 1918 and never knew her mother, who had died in the influenza epidemic shortly after her birth. Her mother's sister raised her. During World War II, my grandmother singlehandedly raised my mom and her siblings while my grandfather fought in the Pacific theater. To make ends meet, my grandmother catered bridge and other social events for more *well to do* ladies. I remembered my grandmother showing me how to make a perfect tea sandwich and serving them on doily-lined silver trays.

I also remembered my aunts, most of whom were war brides married to GIs fighting on the other side of the world from Brooklyn, all of whom had their own careers. I could almost hear their voices as they shared stories about rationing and *making do or doing without* during the war.

As I stood in my dining room looking at the table covered with our family's most precious heirlooms, I realized all of those women loved and lost as I had done that year. And all of them carried on in the face of daunting moments. They passed more than beautiful objects to me: they left me a legacy of resilience and survival.

I took a moment to text Drs. Abbasi and Diehl to thank them for their care, which allowed me to celebrate Thanksgiving that year with the people I loved the most.

The sun glowed in the late fall sky, bathing the ruby dining room in warm light. I lit the candles, and my family gathered at the table. We joined hands and said grace. My voice cracked as I recited the prayers and our intentions: giving thanks for our health, remembering those gone, and offering prayers for my doctors and their families, my sister, and other health care workers separated from their families that day.

We ate and toasted, passing the turkey, stuffing and cranberries around. We told the family stories we've all heard before. The meal ended too soon, and not a crumb of Jeanne's perfectly imperfect lemon meringue pie remained.

After everyone went home, Tim and I began wrapping and packing the leftovers and cleaning up. Ollie emerged from his bed under my desk, happy that the house was quiet again.

Hours later, we collapsed onto the couch in the family room. I pulled my fleecy throw blanket up to my neck and saw a small leather tag on it that I hadn't noticed. *Trust the Journey*, the tag read. It was as if a veil had been lifted from my eyes.

"Oh, shut up," I said.

Tim looked up at me. "What? Are you talking to me?"

"No, not you," I laughed. "It's the tag on the blanket: *Trust the Journey*. That's what I was *supposed* to do all along. How did I not see this until now?"

After a few moments, Tim answered, "Maybe you weren't meant to see it before now."

Tim wasn't much for philosophy or spirituality. He also wasn't a man of many words. But once in a while he saw the world with disarming clarity, which could be equally endearing and annoying. Grace, in its spiritual and ordinary forms, had been ringing my doorbell for months, and the more I ignored it, the louder the bell rang. Grace has its roots in the Latin word, *gratia*, meaning favor, a gift freely given, and came to me in cards and texts, through meals and prayers, on an angel necklace, and even on a blanket. Grace came from different people: my family, my sister, my friends, and my doctors. All I had to do was answer the damn door and welcome *grace* in. This was easier said than done, given how tightly I clung to my need to control my little corner of the universe.

It was time to try.

*Why hello, Grace. Won't you please come in?*

⟡

I'd like to say this karmic-kick-in-the-pants stuck with me in the years following that Thanksgiving evening, that I'd learned my lesson once and for all. Alas, I hadn't. Yet, when I found myself grasping for control, trying to order my life a bit too much, or doubting this new writing life, the doorbell inevitably rang again.

On a few occasions, grace has reintroduced me to old friends at the right moment, and I've renewed friendships I thought were long over. On others, it's helped to send my self-doubt packing by connecting me with the right teacher, the reader, or the right book.

⟡

Two years after I'd finished treatment, I searched my bedroom bookshelves to find *To Know by Experience*, a book that my dad's colleague had given me when I was in the hospital in 1981. I couldn't find the book.

When I had all but given up my search, I saw the book on the lowest shelf in the corner of the bookcase. Sitting cross-legged on the floor, I opened the book to an image of a climber rappelling down a cliff and these words: *once you have looked fear in the face and have overcome it, you can do it again and again.* As I flipped the pages, read the participant's courageous insights, and marveled at the strength of the young men and women in the photographs, I shook my head in disbelief. I felt like Dorothy in *The Wizard of Oz* when she returned to Kansas. Everything I should have known or needed to learn again was here, right in front of me the whole time I was in treatment. But, I didn't think to look for it in a book, though that would have been the most obvious place for me to look.

Too wrapped up in my fear and desire for *normal*, I'd buried all the lessons I'd learned as a teen in the Box.

It was nice of *grace* to remind me that they were there.

⌇

A week after Thanksgiving and the great blanket insight, I had my implant and nipple reconstruction surgery. When I got home, I checked out my new girls in the mirror. All things considered, they looked good. Pert and a little bruised from the procedure, they weren't hard and rigid like the expanders. I wasn't as sore as I'd been after the mastectomy, and I was happy to have reconstructed nipples in the center of my breasts. My areolas still were missing, but they'd be tattooed a few months later after the incisions healed.

Having reconstructed breasts that looked like actual breasts made a huge difference. I felt more like a woman again and less like a doll. I was so thrilled, I posted, *The girls are back in town!* on my Facebook wall.

The next day, Tim and I headed to Madison Square Garden to see Stevie Nicks, my favorite singer of all time. I'd bought the tickets months before the Beast arrived. Nothing, not even breast surgery, would stop me from seeing this concert.

Stevie Nicks stood on stage, still so cool in her velvet platform boots, long, flowing black skirt and cape, and tumble of blonde hair. Her throaty voice rang out over the arena as she performed my favorite songs—the ones that kept me company years ago.

When she sang *Landslide*, I couldn't stop tears. The year's landslide had brought me down to the place where my darkest fears lived.

Yet, I stood.

⌇

After the concert, I rushed headlong into preparations for Christmas. In between decorating the house, wrapping presents, and baking cookies, I still had to go to Dr. Abbasi's for my Herceptin infusion. After our now routine hello hug, review of my labs, and chat about our families, I asked Dr. Abbasi what he thought of what I wrote for Karen.

"When you told me you were writing a list for Karen a couple of months ago, I thought you were going to hand me a handwritten list on a piece of note paper, not this," he said, pulling the document out of his desk drawer. "Chris, this is good. I even asked my daughter, who was an English major, to read it."

"You did *not*, Dr. Abbasi!" I said as my face turned scarlet.

"I did and she loved it. You should publish this."

"Okay, you're sweet, but you should stick to medicine. This isn't anything that could be published. It's the journaling of one cancer patient."

"You should keep working at it."

Intrigued at the thought, I smiled and replied, "Maybe I will then, Dr. Abbasi. Maybe, I will."

The sun hung low in the gray December sky as I drove home. I turned the doctor's words over in my mind. But how would I start? Where would I begin? I smiled to myself as I watched the pale sun dip below the horizon.

I'd begin as I'd always done.

To Do
Write

# Part Three

## CLOSER TO FINE

# Chapter 16
## Getting My Groove Back

To Do
Enroll in writing classes
Find a pretty bra that fits
End the year of the drought

It's January, a few weeks shy of the third anniversary of my breast cancer diagnosis. I stand wrapped in a warm white towel after my post-workout shower. I peer out through the shuttered windows and see the tops of the pines lining our driveway sway in the wind. I run another towel through my hair, then unwrap my now-dry body and let that towel fall to my feet. I stand before the mirror above my vanity.

I no longer look away. I no longer hide under my towel, stay wrapped in a robe, or dress in the semi-dark of my closet. I now have a beautiful pair of pert, well-proportioned breasts that frame the black pin dot radiation tattoo on my chest between them. My scars, once angry crimson streaks, have faded to fine lines of translucent non-color, like a fish's underbelly. They are almost imperceptible.

I slather moisturizer into my parched skin resulting from a combination of age, a daily dose of Tamoxifen, and the winter weather. My hands, filled with softly scented lotion, pass across my chest, but my breasts don't feel my touch. Those nerves were severed during the surgery, another toll exacted by the Beast. Despite the bathroom's steamy warmth, my hands only register my breasts' coolness. It took months to get used to the feeling of the temperature of the skin above the implants being cooler than the surrounding skin. I push my shoulders back and watch my chest rise and fall as I look in the mirror.

I'm no longer shattered by my appearance.

⟶

I relished the weeks leading up to Christmas with the scent of balsam filling the house, the soft light of the candles' glow in each of the windows, and the warm molasses spice cookies that everyone in the family devoured each year. In the past, I often rushed through the season checking off my lists, making sure no one was disappointed with their gifts, and trying to make everything perfect. Not this year. I received the greatest gift, and nothing that came packaged in shiny paper or ribbons could top it.

As I baked or enjoyed time with my kids doing a puzzle or reading together, my mind often returned to Dr. Abbasi's words: that I should keep writing. I prayed daily to see more clearly the path I was meant to take.

In my career as a lawyer, legal writer, and editor, I had worked with some of the best legal writers. I enjoyed my work, but I couldn't bear the thought of going back. If I were to learn that the cancer had returned and I'd spent those precious days enmeshed in employment law, I knew I'd regret it. While I couldn't change where I'd been, I could change where I'd go with my writing skills. I had the luxury—the privilege, to be sure—to chase after the writing dream I'd had since I was a teen. And yet, I hesitated, uncertain whether I had the ability to write creatively or the courage to do something so different than any career I'd ever had.

It would be easier and less risky to go back to law. I didn't know anything about how to become a freelance creative writer, let alone write a book, and I felt like I was standing on a high diving board unable to tell if there was enough water in the pool below me.

During the week between Christmas and New Year's as I dithered about whether to write or try to go back to legal writing, I remembered that a high school friend with whom I'd stayed in touch and who'd made me laugh and smile during my long months of treatment worked in publishing as an editor. I decided to call her and asked for advice on how to go about writing creatively or maybe even starting a book—an advice memoir based off the list I'd written for my nurse.

My friend told me to start with the list and expand it. She also suggested that I take a writing class about how to write memoir or creative non-fiction essays.

"There are tons of classes in New York, Chris. Search online for writing classes or writing programs. I know you'll find something. The other thing you should do is read a website called *Publisher's Lunch* every day, as well as *Nonfiction Book Proposals Anybody Can Write*."

I scrawled notes as Allison talked.

"What's *Publisher's Lunch*?"

"It's a website that lists all the book deals done every day and the authors and agents involved. You can follow it to see what's being published right now. You can see if there are agents who represent authors who are writing books that would be similar to yours."

"That's all very helpful, but I'm a million zillion years from publishing anything. I don't know even know how to write anything, other than a legal brief or an article about some employment law development.

"Well, it doesn't hurt to learn the business side a little at time while you're writing. Chris, you know how to write. You've been doing it for years. All you need to do is sit down and do it. Every day. There's no magic to it. That's what I tell my authors all the time."

"You are, as always, the best, Allison. Thanks."

After our call, I followed her advice and enrolled in classes at Gotham Writer's Workshop in New York City. I began with a one-day memoir and essay writing intensive class. In that marathon eight-hour day, I took one small step toward becoming a writer. I learned the basics of a well-written and constructed narrative, the differences between a memoir and an essay, and more. Our teacher gave us her email and offered her help when class was over.

I walked out knowing I needed to learn a lot more so that I could turn the list I wrote for Karen into a full-length memoir meant to guide other women like me. I wanted to write the book I wanted to read when I was diagnosed and couldn't find. I wanted to write about what it's like to be an ordinary mom faced with this brutal disease, how to care for our loved ones, and how the experience changed my life for good.

On the train ride home to New Jersey, I decided to enroll in a full semester introduction to memoir class that would start in a few weeks' time.

⌣

As I worked through figuring out what to do in my post-cancer life, I also had to learn to live with my post-cancer body—more specifically, my prosthetic breasts. Gone were the days of sleeping on my stomach; now I slept on my back or side because my implants felt like two grapefruits secured to the inside of my chest. Unlike natural breasts, they didn't squish while I was on my stomach. I could feel them all the time on the inside—unlike with my natural breasts, which I never noticed during my day-to-day life. Yet, even though I could feel my implants inside of my body, I had no sensation of them on the outside of my body. My breasts were completely numb.

At the time of the surgery, I didn't think much about the loss of feeling I'd end up with. I was focused on getting the cancer out of my body and doing everything I could to a prevent recurrence. How my breasts would or wouldn't feel afterward was the least of my problems. But, as I recovered and wanted to return to intimacy with Tim, the reality of the loss of sensation in my breasts hit home. That erogenous zone—a big one for me—was gone. I had the memory of Tim's caresses there, but that was all. I grieved that loss deeply.

Even though I couldn't feel Tim's hands any longer on my breasts, I still wanted to look sexy and feminine. But—because with cancer there's always a *but*—none of my pre-surgery bras fit, and I needed a comfortable bra to wear while my incisions fully healed. Why was this a problem? Couldn't I go buy new bras? Or not wear one at all (which was my doctor's suggestion)? While I did choose on occasion to go without because I can, on most days I needed to wear one because my tattooed areolas were visible through lighter fabrics and my reconstructed nipples were permanently erect. As a fifty-year-old mother of teenage boys, I still retained a modicum of modesty, despite baring it all the last year. I wasn't going to be walking around in front of my teenage boys or their friends, running to the grocery store, or sitting at a swim meet without a bra.

*And to all my friends, you're welcome.*

I needed—wanted— to find new lingerie for me, Version 2.0. This proved much harder and frustrating than I imagined. Before surgery, I wore a size 38C, and it was no big deal to shop for a bra. I could always find one that was pretty and comfortable. I had everyday tee-shirt bras, flirty balconettes, and strapless bras. I loved my lingerie. After my surgery, that changed. Bra shopping unexpectedly became more complicated and frustrating. Most bras were wired, and reconstructed breasts didn't need an underwire.

I headed to a local lingerie store. I looked around the bright store filled with racks of lacy, colorful lingerie in pinks, creams, and blacks. I couldn't wait to buy some new underthings. A salesperson showed me to a comfortable fitting room complete with old movie posters and measured me.

"Hmm . . .," she said as she furrowed her brow. "I'll be honest. It's going to be hard to find wireless bras for your shape and size. You are about a 40B, but your implants are lower and wider than your natural breasts were. So, you need to go up a size."

"Up? Up to what?"

"Let's try a 42 or 44C."

I couldn't believe my ears. I knew my new breasts were larger than my originals, but a 44C? I had never worn a bra that large.

As I waited to the salesperson to return, I began to doubt my decision to go bra shopping. After a few minutes, she returned with a stack of hideous bras.

"What *are* these?" I asked, gaping at the big, bulky bras I wouldn't ask my grandma to wear. "Don't you have anything that's, well, you know, pretty? I don't want to wear a Jane Russell bra," I said. My mind flashed back to the television commercials of my teen years where, for reasons that made no sense to me then or now, for that matter, Jane Russell, America's favorite *full-figured gal*, would model functional, supportive, and (always) white bras by hanging them on her arm or wearing them over her sweater.

The saleswoman left me alone with the stack and I made my way through it. I tried on one bra after another and grew more disgusted each time I looked in the mirror at myself. These bras didn't make me feel pretty or feminine like all of my pre-mastectomy lingerie did. I couldn't believe after all the crap I went through I couldn't find a pretty bra that fit. I felt defeated and disheartened at the thought of a future with no lacy lingerie.

"How are we doing?" the saleswoman asked, from outside the cotton curtain.

"Fine," I sighed. "I think I found something that will work, at least."

The plain beige bra in a stretchy fabric, although unattractive, would definitely give my new breasts room to heal. But I wasn't feeling the love. This bra was all function and no fun. Though Tim would never say a word, I could guess what he'd think: *What's with the granny bra, Chris?*

I drove home and tried not to be too grumpy. I told myself that I wouldn't need to wear this bra forever. This bra was another step in the healing process, and once my incisions healed and the swelling went down, I could replace the boring beige with lacy lingerie.

⁓

A month later, I headed to a department store known for its post-surgery bra fittings to see if I could find something better than simply functional. The salesperson measured me and said she wasn't sure if the store carried any wireless bras that would fit, but would check. I found that odd and disappointing, since the store advertised their post-mastectomy fitting program at my doctor's office and at the local hospital, as well as online. I didn't think my reconstruction or breast size was so unusual that finding a bra that fit would be difficult.

She returned with an armful. But, as with my experience a month earlier, the bigger the bra, the uglier it was. I tried on some bralettes, which I loved, but they didn't fit the width of my implants, which lay lower on my chest. The salesperson suggested that I use expander hooks on the bra's closure. At the time, it seemed like a solution: I could have some attractive bras, even if they didn't exactly fit.

By this time, my new ladies had settled in nicely, as all of the post-surgical swelling had dissipated. However, my first functional bra was too big, and the bralettes with the expanders I had attached didn't fit correctly. The shoulder straps didn't stay up, no matter how much I adjusted them. I returned to my local lingerie store hoping to find something pretty. Maybe something pretty that fit well, once and for all?

I met with the salesperson who had helped me a few months earlier. Explaining that it was time for something more than the functional beige bra and the ill-fitting bralettes, I pointed to cute numbers on the racks with lace and in different colors and asked if they came in my size. The salesperson kept shaking her head, "No," and blamed the bra manufacturers for my dilemma. After much back and forth, I was offered two soft bras—in basic white and navy blue—with little bows and a silver charm between the cups. They were not bad looking, but they were not going to light up the night either.

After dancing with cancer for a year, it should have been fun to restock the lingerie drawer.

I left the store, got into my car, and pounded my steering wheel. *Why is this so hard?* Dumb, stupid cancer took my breasts and my loveliest choice of lingerie, too.

I wasn't going to settle for some boring bra. There had to be another option.

And, there was, as I learned a few weeks later when I read an article about a lingerie fashion show that featured models with mastectomies. Some models walked the runway baring it all— whether they were flat or had a lumpectomy, single mastectomy, or bilateral mastectomy. Some models showed off their stunning mastectomy tattoos. And, some of them wore the prettiest bras.

I had found the answer to the lingerie problem that continued to plague me.

⌒

Founded by Dana Donofree, a breast cancer survivor and fashion designer, AnaOno is a lingerie company for women with breast cancer (www.anaono.com). Dana Donofree started the company after she was diagnosed at twenty-seven because, like me, she wanted pretty, sexy, beautiful lingerie after a time in her life that was anything but beautiful.

I found the company's website and went shopping. A few days later, my new bras arrived. They were wireless and fit me perfectly. They came in a rainbow of colors: smoky mauve, navy blue, bright pink, red, ivory, and black. The fabric was lacy, soft, and comfortable. They were beautiful and sexy and made me feel confident, feminine, and whole once more.

I ran to my computer, posted a glowing review, and sent an email to AnaOno, thanking them for designing bras for women like me. Much to my surprise, I received an email from the founder, thanking me for the review and telling me how much she enjoyed receiving notes like mine.

⌣

As February and swimming championship season rolled along, Tom and I found ourselves in another suite-style hotel on a Saturday night in South Jersey with not much to do. I brought along my computer and notebook with my notes from the writing class I'd taken a few weeks earlier. I tried to brainstorm ideas for short essays, but nothing came to mind. I decided to change into my pajamas and read instead, while Tom watched a movie in the living room. As I got undressed, I looked down at my AnaOno bra and thought, *Why not write about my agonizing bra hunt after my mastectomy?*

I got in bed and pulled the computer onto my lap, eager not to lose the thoughts racing though my head. I started an outline of an essay as I sat in the hotel bed, the laptop resting on my knees. I also started asking questions. Why was it difficult to find lingerie for women after breast surgery? Why didn't the traditional manufacturers make bras for women like me? I started researching the answers to those questions until late into the night and long after Tom fell asleep.

Over the next few weeks, I researched and wrote the essay, then emailed my instructor and asked for help on getting it placed for publication with an online magazine, a process called *pitching,* in the writing world. She helped me draft the email to an editor at

Racked.com, an online fashion publication, and it was accepted for publication.

A few months later, when I saw my name with a byline, I couldn't stop smiling. I posted the article on Facebook, and I sent it to Dana Donofree, who was thrilled about it. I also texted it to Dr. Abbasi and emailed it to Karen.

Dr. Abbasi offered his congratulations, then said, "Keep writing, Chris."

Karen asked me if she could share it with her patients in her breast cancer support group.

"Of course," I replied.

⌒

During those winter months, my hair had started to grow in. I didn't feel ugly or awful anymore, and I wanted to return to intimacy with my husband. My plan to end the year of the drought did not go as desired, however, because nothing was easy or simple with surviving cancer. Not even sex.

When we first made love about a month after my implant surgery, Tim kissed me, gently moving from my face, to my ears, neck and upper chest. I felt the rush of heat move from my stomach to my pelvis. I pulled Tim toward me and felt the warmth of his breath on my neck.

"Can I . . .?" Tim asked, gesturing to my breasts.

"Of course, they're not going to pop," I laughed.

"I want to make sure you're fine with it."

"You're sweet, and yes, it's totally fine."

I watched as Tim's hands moved across my breasts. And, I felt nothing. My spine stiffened.

"What's wrong?" Tim asked. His face belied his trepidation.

I remembered how easy and comfortable our sex life had been, as if our bodies were made for each other. But now my body felt like a stranger—the deepest of betrayals.

"It's weird. I can't feel anything," I admitted, even though I didn't want to ruin this night.

"Do you want me not to touch you?" Tim asked as he leaned up on his elbow.

"No, no, of course not."

"You are always beautiful to me," he said as he traced his fingers along my cheekbone, "but if it makes you unhappy, then I'll let them be."

I sat up and pulled the comforter around me.

"It's strange. I knew this would happen. I mean, that's what my doctors told me. But it's one thing to know something, and it's something else to experience it. Do you know what I mean?"

He nodded. We lay in silence. I rested my head on Tim's chest and breathed in the scent of him as he rubbed my cheek.

"I can feel sensation above my breasts," I said.

"Well, let's start there then."

We started over, and I held onto my memories of what I used to feel as his hands passed over my chest. We made quiet, gentle love for the first time in months.

The next morning, I was surprised at how sore my vagina was. Reflecting on the night, I realized that, as wonderful as it was to make love again, it took me forever to have an orgasm.

*You'd think that after not having sex for months, it would have taken twenty seconds. It's the damn Tamoxifen, I know it.*

While Tamoxifen was great for preventing recurrence of breast cancer, it did a number on my sex life—which shouldn't have been surprising, since Tamoxifen suppresses estrogen. I now needed a solution to the lack of a sex drive and bone-dry vagina I was experiencing.

During my annual gynecological exam, I explained the situation to my doctor, who had been my gynecologist for fifteen years.

"Let's get you back on the wagon, Chris, because at our age, a good sex life is one of best things we have left," my doctor said after hearing my symptoms.

"You've got that right," I laughed.

My doctor left the exam room and returned with a low dose estrogen cream in hand, and told me to use it with plenty of high-quality personal lubricant.

"Get as sloppy as you'd like, but . . ." my doctor paused.

*Because nothing was easy or simple with cancer.*

"You need to clear the prescription estrogen cream with Dr. Abbasi."

"Oh my gosh, can't you text him or something? This isn't a conversation I want to have with him. I will die of embarrassment."

"He's your oncologist, Chris. You can to talk to him."

I left shaking my head in disbelief. I couldn't imagine having that conversation with my conservative, professorial oncologist.

⌒

A few weeks later, while Dr. Abbasi and I had our pre-infusion schmooze about our families, I reached into my purse and pulled out my box of estrogen cream. I'd decided I would slide it across the desk and ask him to tell me thumbs-up or thumbs-down—a creative solution to an awkward conversation.

As I pulled the box from my purse, the tube fell out of the box and rolled under his desk. I reached down as discretely as I could, which is to say, not at all.

"Is everything all right, Chris?"

"Yes, but I have to ask you about this," I said, straightening myself up in the chair and smiling my brightest smile. "Can I use this? My gynecologist told me to clear it with you," I said, sliding the empty box across the desk.

He reached for it and examined the label.

"Oh, do you have vaginal dryness? You know, there were studies when these creams first came out questioning whether they would impact Tamoxifen's effectiveness, but it's such a low dose that . . ."

I cut his lecture short, turning scarlet as I did.

"Dr. Abbasi, all I want to know is—can we improve my quality of life? Thumbs-up or thumbs-down to this?"

He smiled at me.

"Yes, of course, by all means, use it as you need, and tell Tim *Happy New Year!*"

"Tell Tim? I believe you meant me," I said, and winked as I left his office for my infusion.

Thumbs-up, it was.

⌒

It took time to get used to using the cream and remembering to *get sloppy* anytime Tim and I wanted to make love. But, as with most of life after cancer, Tim and I got used to it. Neither of us wanted to spend the life we'd been given back together as celibates.

We took our time—a year or two—learning how my new body responded. We worked to make it work, but not all cancer patients and their partners are as lucky as I am.

⌒

I began to wonder if other women experienced similar problems. At the time, I couldn't find candid articles about sex after cancer, although I looked for them. Today, that's changing: Living Beyond Breast Cancer regularly includes sexual health and wellness webinars on their site (www.lbbc.org). Books have been written about it (please see *Resources*). The topic has become less taboo, but when I was searching in late 2016, the articles I found were either too clinical or spent a great deal of time discussing men's sexual dysfunction after prostate cancer. While important to discuss, that topic didn't apply to me.

I decided to talk to other women survivors. I contacted Nora, an ovarian cancer survivor and one of the founders of CancerGrad.com. Nora had reposted my article about the great bra hunt on CancerGrad's blog and Facebook page, so I thought she might help.

She agreed to discuss her experience and suggested that I post my request to talk on CancerGrad's Facebook page. I learned much from those conversations.

Sexuality can change profoundly because of cancer treatment. In addition to the loss of the breasts and the loss of sensation in them, breast cancer patients often experience other less obvious losses. Women whose ovaries are removed or who need certain hormonal therapies may experience early menopause, with all of its attendant symptoms, like hot flashes, sweating, and mood swings. These therapies also have other side effects, such as the loss of sexual desire or vaginal dryness that makes sexual intercourse painful or impossible.

For young breast cancer patients, the impact on their sex lives can be challenging for them and their partners given the common loss of sexual desire. Another challenge is fertility loss, which may occur in two ways: first, the cancer may affect the reproductive system directly, and, second, cancer treatment, including chemotherapy, radiation, and surgery, can damage the reproductive system. Hormonal therapy also can induce menopause, which ends ovulation.

Nora was diagnosed with ovarian cancer at thirty-nine. When ovarian cancer is suspected, the woman must undergo surgery to diagnose the disease. When Nora awoke following this surgery, her husband broke the news to her that, yes, she had ovarian cancer, and yes, her ovaries and uterus had been removed. Upon hearing this news, Nora felt like a rug had pulled out from under her. She had lost a big part of what made her a woman.

Depending on a woman's age, she may not regain her fertility after treatment. While there are a growing number of ways to preserve fertility in the face of a cancer diagnosis—such as egg and embryo freezing—these treatments are costly and typically not covered by health insurance. These factors prove difficult to consider, particularly for younger women who may not have contemplated parenthood and who may not be able to afford the treatment at all.

When faced with the surgery to determine if she had ovarian cancer, Nora and her husband had only a few minutes to decide whether to harvest her eggs for a subsequent surrogate pregnancy. Nora hadn't planned on having children, but when confronted with the reality she might not be able have them, she began questioning her decision. Although she chose not to preserve her eggs, she grieved that cancer took the choice from her. It was no consolation to hear well-meaning friends or relatives say, "At least you didn't want to have children." Even today, years after her surgery, Nora still grieves the loss of her ability to change her mind and choose something different for her life.

Grief, like a scar, fades over time, but it never disappears.

# Chapter 17
## After *The End*

To Do
Celebrate *The End*
Get back to the gym
Spring clean garden
England

ON THIS MID-FEBRUARY MORNING, snow traces the branches of the cedars and maple trees surrounding our terrace. With my kids off to school, Ollie walked, and my spin class done, I sit at my desk with yesterday's drafts ready for my pencil. The mornings move with a mellow rhythm now that the days of running to doctor's appointments have faded, if not completely from view, with enough distance to make them seem like the dim edge of a forest. Now I write. I'm doing exactly what I set out to do when my treatment ended.

I cherish these quiet hours.

One of my teachers said we must write about what we most want to avoid because it has the most power over us. We have to open that cellar door and go down into the dark, cobweb-filled spaces and pull the cord for the light bulb to illuminate the dusty old boxes sitting in the corner of our memory. I'd like to say that once treatment ended, my life returned to normal. I closed the breast cancer chapter, stuck it in the Box, shoved it in the basement, and moved on. But with cancer—and as you now know, with cancer there's always a *but*—that's not what happened.

While part of me wanted to get back to normal life like I thought I had after my Hodgkin's, part of me also knew, and perhaps had known since my teenage years, I had buried my fear of cancer and its recurrence—of the Beast. My fears wouldn't lose their grip over me until I faced them. To reclaim my life, I had to open the cellar door and step into the dark.

I only knew how to do that one way: through words. And this time, I wouldn't throw them away.

At my last Herceptin appointment, Dr. Abbasi finalized my chart, embraced me, and told me he'd see me in three months. In return, I gave him a copy of Oliver Sacks' collection of essays, *Gratitude*, which Sacks wrote shortly before he succumbed to cancer. In it, he summed up his feelings about reaching the end of his brilliant life as a physician and writer, noting that more than anything else, he felt a sense of gratitude for his life.

I had similar feelings about reaching the end of treatment. I was overwhelmed with gratitude that I'd made it through and received so much. I knew I wanted to give something back. I didn't know what exactly, but something. I also wanted to travel someplace special to celebrate *The End* as well as my twenty-fifth wedding anniversary.

Tim and I decided after all the treatment was over, we would focus on doing more things together, like traveling or going to the theater or to concerts. We could do that now much more easily, after years of having to put such things off because of the kids' ages, as well as their activities and the associated costs. We didn't want to keep waiting for the next day or the next year because we knew how quickly and unexpectedly life could change, how on one day I was healthy and on the next, I wasn't. We both knew it could happen again to either or both of us.

But notwithstanding that we made these plans, something nagged at me. Something I couldn't put my finger on. I knew I should be happy, and I was. Sort of. But I also felt uneasy and worried, as I did when I had my last appointment with Dr. Forte and he told me he didn't need to see me anymore. And while I understood that Dr. Abbasi didn't need to see me every three weeks, I felt unmoored, even though it would be years before I'd stop seeing Dr. Abbasi.

*Who will tell me I am okay if Dr. Abbasi doesn't see me every few weeks?*

*"Stop, Christine, just stop. You're fine,"* I said to myself, slamming the lid of the Box down again.

I pushed my unease away—again—as I drove home from my appointment with Dr. Abbasi. I was looking forward to a night out with Tim, Athena, and her husband. I could think of no better way to celebrate the end of treatment than with Athena whose friendship, care, and no-nonsense personality had sheltered me those many days.

Later that evening, we met at Lorena's, a French bistro nearby to celebrate. Champagne chilled in an ice bucket near our perfectly set table, draped with heavy cream-colored linens. Athena's diamonds sparkled in the candlelight, and she wore a round jade pendant that seemed to glow next to her black dress. We toasted The End and our friendship, then shared an exquisite meal together, complete with a half-dozen oysters on the half shell for me, and foie gras for Athena—

two of our favorite dishes. When the night ended and we headed home, my heart was full, and I offered a silent prayer of thanksgiving for the joy of a shared meal.

During the next few weeks, friends and family commented on how great I must feel now that it was *all over*. I did feel great. How could I not? I didn't have to go for infusions any longer. I returned to all my normal activities, like volunteering for the high school PTO and for Tom's swim teams, and the day-to-day stuff of my life, like cooking, running errands, and doing laundry. I also could go back to the gym, and Athena made sure I did, as she outlined her plan for my new exercise routine while we walked together one early April morning.

With the mulch and leaves crunching under our feet, we strode over the damp trails in a local park still wearing our fleeces and gloves. Soon, we wouldn't need those winter layers as we walked. The constant sense of fatigue that plagued me for months had dissipated. I breathed in the cool air and took quiet pleasure in the morning peace. Athena's voice broke my reverie.

"What would you say about coming to spin class again and a core strength workout with me? It's early so I can get to work on time."

"How early? I need to drop the boys at school. And, I'm not sure about the gym yet. My hair has barely filled in. And I'm so out of shape."

"The classes are at 8:00 a.m. so it would be after you drop the boys. You need to get back to it, Chris. Nobody cares about your hair. You're never going to get in shape if you don't start."

"I know, I know. It's just hard. The walking and weight lifting I've done over the last year helped, but it's not the same as a spin class."

"Chris, that is not hard. Do you know what was hard? Cancer. You did that. You can go to an exercise class with me."

I walked, mulling over Athena's words. She was right. I needed to get back to more serious exercise to regain the stamina I'd lost over the last year.

Before breast cancer, I loved to spin. There was no good reason not to go back to it. I could go at my own pace. I knew the instructors; there'd be no judgment there.

I started with one spin class and one core class. I watched my heart rate monitor as my heart raced in my chest. I huffed and puffed my way through those first few weeks with Athena and other friends whom I hadn't seen in over a year. Because Athena met me at the gym, I showed up. She pushed me to do more and told me how proud she was whenever I left my comfort zone and tried a more challenging class. Any time I wanted to quit or not go at all, I reminded myself that, when my life was spinning out of control while I was in treatment, I didn't give up on myself then. I wouldn't give up on myself now as I made my new routine a habit.

As the months and miles on the spin bike passed and my strength and cardiovascular stamina—even my hair—slowly began to return, I found I could exercise five to six days per week until I felt almost stronger than I was before my diagnosis. At the end of our classes while we were cooling down, one of my spin instructors often reminded us to be grateful for the privilege of coming to class. We were the lucky ones sitting hot and sweaty on bikes every Friday morning.

Whenever I heard her speak these words, I nodded and smiled. I paused and silently gave thanks that I was able to get on that bike day after day and week after week.

⌒

A few days after my walk with Athena and after I returned to the gym with her, I stood at my back door looking out over the wreck of my garden. A few wispy clouds hung in a pale blue sky, and the early April sun bathed the yard with cool light. Winter hadn't been kind to my flower beds, nor had my neglect during the past season. Twigs and branches littered the lawn. The redbuds and beautyberry shrubs had grown into one another, a tangled mess of gangly branches. The clethra and lilac had grown lanky. Large swaths where spring bulbs should have started to poke through the soil lay bare, the bulbs probably victim to squirrels and voles.

"Well, standing here looking at the mess isn't going to make it better," I mused aloud. I dug through the closet for my rain boots and jacket. I stuck a pen and notebook in my jacket's pocket and went out to my potting bench in the corner of the garage for my garden pruners.

Like the yard, the bench bore the detritus of neglect: empty grass seed bags, seed packets from last year's vegetable garden, bags of potting soil, and unwashed pots stacked in no particular order—a project for another day. I rummaged around the bench until I found my shears, snug in their leather cover. They needed to be oiled and sharpened, but they'd have to do for now. I stuck them in my pocket and with Ollie at my heel, opened the garden gate and walked through the beds to take stock of what was needed.

Pausing and kneeling down in the cool earth, I brushed away the leaves and mulch to look for sprouts. I saw grape hyacinths and daffodils poking their way through the earth. I made notes of what needed raking and mulching and the low bush shrubs that needed pruning and shaping. I walked along our back border and found the Cornelian cherry starting to bloom—the first harbinger of spring in my garden. Yellow buds lined its branches. All it needed was a few more days of sunshine, and the sulfurous yellow blossoms would shine in that corner of the garden.

These small moments of beauty startled me right now with their intensity. I was seeing the world with new eyes, with sharper clarity than I'd experienced earlier in my life. I began to understand what *living in the moment*—being present even for the smallest experiences that make up our lives—meant.

I snipped a few branches to bring inside and force the blooms. After having reviewed my garden's state of affairs and become sufficiently chilled and muddy, I left my boots at the back door and returned to the kitchen to make a cup of tea.

A mug of warm tea in hand, I made a list of garden chores for the upcoming weekend and plans to head to the nursery. I would plant the urns and planters with yellow, orange, and blue pansies. I loved the look of their smiling flower faces as they danced in the spring breezes.

When I arrived at my favorite nursery a few days later, Amy, the manager who kept me in flowers during the long year before, asked if I needed them to plant for me that year.

"No, I'm happy to do it myself. I'm done with my treatment. I'm happy to be back in my garden again."

"Let us know if you need help cleaning out the beds or with plants, okay?"

"Absolutely. The garden's a bit of a wreck at the moment, so when I start to sort it, I'll let you know."

I loaded my car with the pansies and fresh potting soil, then spent the rest of the afternoon planting the urns and planters, filling them with fresh soil and arranging the happy-faced flowers in each. The bright blue and yellow went in the front of the house, and the sunny tangerine and yellow were in the urns on the patio. I would smile whenever I looked out my kitchen window.

As I watered the last of the planters, brushed away the soil from my jeans, pulled off my work gloves, and stretched my back, I smiled to myself. I'd done it *myself*—another small victory, another step toward normal.

Along with my workouts and spending time outside in my gardens, I also started helping other women who were either recently diagnosed with breast cancer or dealing with family members who were recently diagnosed with cancer. I didn't do this because I wanted to, to be honest. Although I'd reached out to a few friends whom I knew had gone through it for advice and guidance, I never imagined that anyone would turn to *me* for advice, let alone for advice less than a month after I'd finished my last Herceptin infusion. But then my phone rang one afternoon while I was waiting to pick up James from school. I glanced at my phone, and the caller ID showed it was a friend with whom I hadn't spoken in a while.

"Hey Bonnie, what's going on?" I asked.

"Chris, it's Richard," she said, her voice breaking. "He's just been diagnosed with cancer, and I don't know what to do."

I could hear her hiccupping down her tears.

"Oh sweetie, I am so sorry to hear this news. How are you doing? Tell me what's going on."

I listened while Bonnie explained her husband's preliminary diagnosis and possible treatment options. Bonnie started to sob in earnest.

"I'm so scared. What if he dies? What am I going to do?"

"I know. It's scary and awful, and it's okay to be scared," I said, trying to fight my own tears now welling up that someone I knew and cared for had to face the Beast. I breathed deeply and pushed my fear aside: I'd stay in control for her. After all, she called me because of what I knew from my experience, just like I had when I called my friends. In that moment, a wave of calm passed over me. I knew what I needed to say.

"Listen to me. This is what I can tell you based on my experience. You're going to take everything one step at a time. You'll meet with his doctors. You'll consider all the treatment options. So just breathe and try to stay calm."

"How did you stay as calm as you sound?"

"I didn't. But I became a big fan of the occasional Xanax. And, I prayed a lot. Bonnie, the whole diagnosing and planning process takes a while because they have to get it right. You can't really rush the process, and it can be maddening. There's a lot of hurry up, then wait. Try not to make yourself crazy playing the what-if game while the docs figure it out. I can say that, you know, because I'm a master of it."

Bonnie laughed, then took a deep breath, sighed, and shared her next worry.

"But, how do we tell the kids? I don't want to tell them while they're away at college, and we're not even sure what the treatment will be. Richard still has to have more tests. And he doesn't want to tell them at all."

My stomach flipped, and I broke into a cold sweat. I was the last person anyone should consult on this particular cancer question. I did such a poor job telling my own kids. I did the only thing I could think of at the time.

"Well, I can tell you from my experience with Katie that not telling your college-age kids what's going on is a terrible idea. You need to be honest with them even though your instinct is to protect them. They're adults and should know what's up, even if you don't have the whole story yet."

"What did you tell your kids?" Bonnie asked.

I explained I'd wanted to tell my kids when we had all of the information about my diagnosis and treatment, just like she and Richard wanted. Then, I recounted the swim meet weekend miscommunication debacle.

"We made a huge mistake about how we told Katie. I regret it to this day. It's making me sick talking about it. I should have filled her in as I learned the information," I said as I clenched my fist against my stomach. "In my view, you should tell them what you know, when you know it. Then everyone is on the same page."

"Oh Chris, I had no idea about what you went through with Katie."

"I did what I did to protect her at that time, but it just blew up in my face and caused her a great deal of pain. I guess what I'm trying to say is that you can't protect them from this, Bonnie, no matter how much you want to. The truth always finds the day, you know?"

I sat in silence, waiting for Bonnie's response.

"Thanks for telling me all that. You gave me a lot to think and talk about with Richard.

"Let me know how it goes. I'm sorry you have to through this.

James is almost to the car, so I have to go. I don't want him to hear any of this."

"No, of course not. I appreciate talking to you, Chris. It's helped a lot."

"Any time, my friend. You call or text me anytime you need, okay?"

"Yeah," Bonnie replied, and I could hear her trying to swallow her tears again.

"I promise you, sweetie, you'll get through this, even if it doesn't seem so now. You will."

"Really?"

"Really, really," I answered as James opened the door. "Oh, here's James, I'll talk to you soon."

I ended the call and clenched the steering wheel in my fists. I felt like I was about to puke. I hoped James didn't notice as I asked him about his school day and homework until we got home.

As soon as I walked in the house, I texted Dr. Abbasi to ask him why I would be receiving cancer phone calls from friends already. I wasn't prepared. Were they going to be a regular occurrence in my life now?

With his normal aplomb, he answered, *Yes, this is how it will be. And God grant you the strength and health to do it. These are not random people coming your way.*

*Great.*

I sighed and kept reading as he continued to text me. Dr. Abbasi explained these calls reminded him of tokens for a game machine. I needed to keep adding tokens to it to let the game continue.

Even better. Now my own life depended on playing the game— metaphorically speaking.

The calls, texts, and emails started coming one at time, week after week, while I walked Ollie, while I was swim meets with Tom, or during breakfast and dinner. They all began the same way: *I just found out . . . I was just diagnosed . . . My friend just heard and needs someone to talk to. Can I give her your number?*

And, each time it happened, I listened. I answered questions. I gave people my number. I shared my experiences. The calls, the texts, and the emails—too many to count now—allowed me to return the many graces I received while I was in treatment. I now viewed those conversations as a form of karmic payback or the closing of a great cosmic loop—Dr. Abbasi's game tokens, so to speak.

*Because this is how it is.*

⌒

In late April, a few weeks after my phone call with Bonnie, I began a semester-long introduction-to-memoir class. I wrote essays and scenes, submitted them for critique, and held my breath while waiting to get my teacher's comments back.

On other days, I participated in workshops. For those who have never participated in a writer's workshop, as I had not, this form of perdition entailed having everyone else in my class read my work then give constructive feedback on the piece while I sat silently until it was over. In the greater scheme of things, I'd rate the experience as better than having cancer or a root canal—but not by much.

After I got over the initial shock, self-loathing, and intellectual bruising involved in a writing workshop, I summoned the courage on the following day to read the edited, red-lined version of my work, now filled with notations and comments from the instructor. After I finished reading, I put my head down on my arms, folded on top of my desk and stared into the dark.

*What are you doing, Christine? You suck at this. You could go back to law and legal writing. It wouldn't be anywhere near as hard as this.*

After I stood up and shook off my shock, I skulked down the hall and into Tim's office, flopped on the chair and sighed.

"I have no business trying to write a book."

Tim looked up from his computer. "Stop that. Why? What happened?"

I waved my redlined and heavily edited pages at him. "This."

"Put it down for a bit. Take Ollie for a walk. Call Athena. Then, get back to it when you're not smarting."

"It's not that easy, Tim."

"Go over the comments and suggestions and start again. That's the only way to do it. You know this."

"Ugh. I hate it when you're right."

Tim walked over to me and gave me a hug.

"You can do this. Now, out. I have to get on a call," he said as he nudged me out of his office.

Using the instructor's comments and writing exercises, I took the original list of things I knew now and worked at expanding it into a story. I added dialogue and created scenes. I submitted my work each week to my instructor and rewrote my pieces over and over.

⌐⌐

When I needed a break from the computer and my cancer memories, I returned to my gardening, as spring blossomed toward summer. And yet, in the face of all this delicious normalcy and small moments of joy, freedom, and creativity, the feeling of unease crept up on me when I least expected it. I could be in my garden or at the grocery store, and my mind would go blank. I'd have to stop and refocus on what I was doing.

*Just cut the daffodils and bring them inside.*

*Milk—put it in the cart.*

It made no sense. I knew that I was well, but I couldn't shake the lingering fear that it was just a matter of time until I wouldn't be again.

As time drew near for my first post-treatment appointment with Dr. Abbasi in June, my unease worsened. During chemotherapy and following my surgery, my doctors, nurses, and other health care professionals had wrapped me a cocoon of care—day after day, week after week, month after month. I had focused on *getting through it* with all of their support. Now that treatment had ended, the cocoon unraveled, and I felt bare, unprotected. Tension filled me. I walked around with an icy knot in my chest, but I didn't want to talk about how I felt. I thought no one would understand why I couldn't just *be normal*.

At two in the morning, I lay in bed playing the *what if* game again ...

*What if it comes back? What if I have to have chemo again?*

*Your pathology report was excellent, Christine. You're taking Tamoxifen. You're doing everything you can reasonably do to stay healthy.*

*But it can come back, though, no matter what I do. And, it could kill me.*

*Stop. Talk to Dr. Abbasi when you see him. Now, say a Hail Mary and go back to sleep.*

My internal stress and lack of sleep affected everyone else in the family, although I didn't realize it at the time—much like I didn't realize how poorly I acted when I was in treatment. However, one Saturday afternoon as I stood at the top of our staircase, a conversation between Tom and Tim drifted up the stairs. I glanced down. I could see Tim's door slightly open, and Tom, sitting in a chair across from his desk. Even with his back to me, I could make out his words.

"What is up with Mom? She lost her shit with me because I didn't put my dishes in the dishwasher. She went on and on about how selfish I was and how she's not my maid and everything."

I couldn't believe what I heard.

*I wasn't really being that short with Tom. Besides, he should have put his dishes in the dishwasher.*

"Well, she's not your maid, Tom. But you're right, she's been short with everyone this week. I think she's nervous because . . ."

Tim's voice lowered, and I couldn't make out his words.

When I finally saw Dr. Abbasi, relief flooded over me. The icy knot in my stomach faded, and I allowed my shoulders to drop as I breathed out the stress I'd been holding for the past few weeks.

After our hello hug, he checked my blood tests and reassured me that I was fine. I told him how nervous I'd been lately and how I couldn't sleep. Dr. Abbasi told me that anxiety was common after going through treatment and it would take time to heal emotionally as well as physically. He also reminded me that I responded well to my treatment, as I knew from having read and reread my surgical pathology report.

"I know all this, Dr. Abbasi. But, I can't stop myself from worrying, and I don't want to live in fear all the time," I said as I held my hands together.

"You have to give yourself time, Chris. You can't control the future. It's not in your hands," he replied, gesturing toward the ceiling.

I smiled at him and understood that he was telling me to leave the future to God.

"I know. I know. I never imagined it would be this hard," I sighed.

"It's hard because you're trying to control something that you can't. I want you to enjoy your upcoming trip to England with your family. Celebrate with them there—they're most important, after all. This is a happy time for you. So try not to worry about that which is not in your hands."

I nodded. I knew he was right.

*Again.*

The tension further left my neck and shoulders as I walked out of the Simon Center. My breathing slowed. My heart stopped racing.

*I don't have cancer. I don't have cancer. I don't have cancer.*

I repeated my new mantra to myself on the drive home. I pushed the thought of the possibility into the Box and focused on the trip abroad.

A week later, we left for England. My family and I visited perfect English gardens, hiked through grassy fields, and walked through medieval cathedrals, Roman ruins, and country towns. We roamed through museums. We enjoyed pub lunches sitting at time-worn wooden tables surrounded by whitewashed walls as the boys tucked into fish and chips doused with vinegar. I basked in the moments, grateful that the care I received allowed me to have them at all.

Tim and I had made it through some of the hardest days of our marriage that year, so we quietly celebrated our anniversary on our last night in London at Veeraswamy Restaurant, England's oldest classical Indian restaurant, overlooking Regent Street. I chose Veeraswamy not only because Tim and I love Indian food, but also because we celebrated our engagement with our parents twenty-six years before at Nirvana, an Indian restaurant in New York City.

We walked into the dining room decorated with ornate screens and colorful glass chandeliers. Rose petals were scattered on each table. When we sat down, a chilled bottle of champagne awaited us—a gift from Tim's colleagues with a note wishing us a happy anniversary.

"Oh my gosh, Tim. They all did so much for us. This is over the top."

"I work with good people. They had to jump through a couple of hoops to make this happen."

"You knew about it? Stinker!"

"I wanted it to be a surprise for you."

"Here's to twenty-five more years together," we said as our glasses clinked.

⌒

When we returned home from England, summer fell into its sweet, slow rhythm. James went off to Boy Scout camp in the Adirondacks in July. Tom had a job lifeguarding at a local pool club. Katie had an internship working in a homeless shelter in Vermont.

I started my second semester-long memoir writing class that ended in mid-September after everyone was back in school.

Like the first class, I had readings, writing assignments, and workshops. My instructor spent several weeks on *alternative points of view*, or how other people—characters—perceived the events. As another writing instructor explained, *Every villain is the hero in his or her own story*. Notwithstanding that I'd seen the Broadway musical, *Wicked*, years before and loved it—it retells *The Wizard of Oz* from the perspective of the Wicked Witch—I didn't understand how important others' points of view were until I took this class. Until then, the story was all about me.

I spent many of my days at my computer or on my laptop at the pool club where Tom worked, trying to apply what I learned to what I'd written, adding in my family's perspective to the story.

But at the oddest, random moments, fear of recurrence of disease overtook my rational mind. I couldn't stop worrying that the cancer would return. I couldn't reconcile what Dr. Abbasi had told me about my positive response to treatment with the icy cold fear that deep inside of me the Beast stilled lurked, waiting to strike again.

I wondered if my fears and feelings were unique. My gut told me they weren't, but I had to find out. Again applying the lessons I'd learned about alternative points of view, I decided I needed to talk to other survivors to find out before I could write about life after treatment. To do that, I first turned to Dana Donofree since she was well-connected in the young survivor community. I sent her an email to ask whether she'd be willing to talk to me about her experiences and if she knew anyone else who might be willing to speak with me.

Within a day of my request, Dana sent emails to several other survivors, some of whom had appeared in her fashion shows, to ask if they'd mind speaking with me. A few days later, I'd arranged phone calls with Dana and two other women: Rachel, a tie designer from California, and Melissa, a school principal from New Jersey.

Calling on my background as an attorney, I developed a list

of questions like I would have done for any witness interview. In particular, I focused on how breast or other cancers change one's body image; how breast cancer changed one's feminine identity; and how life after cancer looked. For the balance of that summer, I conversed with these women in person, by phone, and online.

⌒

I chatted with Dana on a warm July afternoon as I waited in my car to meet Katie after she finished her workday at the homeless shelter in rural Vermont. Dana spoke with authority as she told her story.

On the day before her twenty-eighth birthday, Dana was diagnosed with breast cancer and later underwent chemotherapy and surgery. She decided to have a bilateral mastectomy, although the tumor was in one breast. Like me, she knew she wouldn't be able to handle the stress of screenings every six months on the remaining side. She also was afraid of dealing with a recurrence. She also received similar lectures from surgeons about prophylactic mastectomies and survival rates. Her response to her doctors was similar to mine: *Don't blame me for wanting to limit my stress. I have to live this life. And living life* is *the journey*!

I asked Dana about how she felt about her body and her femininity after her surgery. Dana told me no longer felt feminine or whole, but *diced, sliced and confused.* Like me, she would not take off her clothes in front of her partner after her mastectomy.

"We feel vulnerable around those we love the most," Dana explained. "Breast surgery causes a deconstruction of the self."

When Dana told me, "I straight up lost myself," I felt a kinship with her that I hadn't experienced previously.

I wasn't alone, and I wasn't crazy. I'd experienced many of the same emotions and conversations that she'd had.

Dana's emotional responses to her post-cancer body and to her appearance led to the creation of AnaOno. She wanted a *beautiful dressing* to cover her scars and feel sexy again. She had been wearing sports bras and tee shirts, and she was tired of not being able to wear a dress or a dressy blouse.

"What was the point, if nothing fit correctly?" she told me.

Since she'd worked in the fashion industry, she decided to create her own line of lingerie for breast cancer patients and survivors. One of her proudest moments occurred when she could wear the blouse she wanted to wear.

"I felt like me again," she said.

"Oh my gosh, Dana. That's all I wanted after my surgery. I just wanted to wear a bra that made me feel like me," I replied.

If she could recreate her life after surgery, maybe I could do the same thing.

⁓

After my long weekend visit with Katie and then return to Vermont a week later to bring her home because she was sick, I spoke with more survivors about their lives after treatment. I talked with Melissa, a school principal and mom.

I wasn't surprised to hear that she still experienced anxiety about cancer even though her treatment had ended several years ago. She told me her anxiety became more intense as the time for her six-month checkups grew near. Melissa told me that she stopped trying to explain it to her family and friends; they thought it was *all over*. But it wasn't for her.

"It's almost as though I need someone to tell me I don't have cancer, every day," she said as she exhaled into the phone.

"So what do you do about it?" I asked.

Melissa said that she saw a professional therapist, and she got involved in a charity supporting other survivors. She also started her own business and obtained her principal's certification in an accelerated twelve-month program.

"I was too much in my head. I had to get out," she confided.

"I get that. Melissa. I totally get that."

After I hung up my phone, I lay my head on my arms. I understood how she felt. Even as I tried to piece my life back together, I had to come to terms with cancer's dirty little secret: the Beast can always return and morph—a shape-shifting shadow—into a new or metastatic disease, one with no cure, one that could, next time, end my life. So, how would I live with this knowledge? I decided I would keep talking with other survivors, including Rachel, a breast cancer survivor from Los Angeles.

⌣

Rachel spoke with the forthrightness that came from experience. I felt as if she'd asked herself many of the questions I had for her. When I asked her what the hardest part about having breast cancer was, she surprised me with her answer. She explained that the greatest misconception about cancer is that treatment is the hardest part.

"It's not," Rachel said. "When I got to the finish line, I had to ask myself what life after cancer looked like."

After treatment, Rachel had to get *comfortable being uncomfortable*—meaning she had to learn to live with the lingering anxiety about recurrence. And she promised herself that she would no longer do things that she didn't want to do.

Rachel realized that she had a chance to re-invent herself and live a more authentic, meaningful life. So, in addition to designing bespoke ties, she started a new business and created a portable, chest-comforting pillow that attaches directly to a seat belt to protect the chest after breast surgery or from skin discomfort caused by radiation therapy.

"Rachel, that was genius. I had these little baby doll style pillows I received in the hospital, but they never stayed put. What a great solution."

As we wound down our conversation, Rachel asked me what I planned to do in my life after cancer.

"I'm planning to write an essay based on these interviews. I think I also want to write a book, but that's going to take time."

"I can't tell you what to do, Chris. But I can tell you, just *start!* Life is too short. It's never going to be perfect. Whatever you want to do, do it now. Tomorrow is never promised."

"That's great advice, Rachel, and I will include it in whatever I write. Thank you."

After speaking with Dana, Melissa, and Rachel, I felt more at ease. My fear, anxiety and desire to reassess my life and what I was doing with it seemed common enough among survivors.

Rachel's words stayed in my head. I needed to teach myself how to live with the *uncomfortable*.

To do that, I had to keep writing. I also had to give something back to the faith community who had lifted me up over the past year, with prayers, meals, and the delivery of Holy Communion when I was too sick to go to church. I became a Eucharistic Minister and now do the same for others who are sick or homebound.

## The Practical Reality
### Advice-Giving From Those Who Are Patients, Survivors and Caregivers

Whenever someone who was recently diagnosed or whose family member was recently diagnosed asks me for advice, I tell her how saddened I am to hear the news, and that it sucks. I then ask the person what I can do for her or what she needs.

After this, I listen. If she asks me specific questions, I try to use *I* statements, not *you* statements. What I mean by this is that I share *my* experience and tell her what I know or what I personally found helpful on my path to recovery. I try not to say, *you should* or *you must* because I don't know what her doctors will tell her about her experience, health, and situation.

We're all different, and so what we and our bodies need, and what our doctors recommend for us, are likely to differ. Also, advances and changes in cancer treatment and protocols occur often, so what I experienced in 2016 probably isn't what's current today.

**Dry Mouth**

In addition to messing with my sense of taste, chemotherapy also altered my mouth's chemistry so now I have a bone-dry mouth. If you find that your mouth is unusually dry as you recover from chemotherapy, speak to your dentist to develop a care plan, but here's what worked for me.

I use a hydrating mouthwash, such as Biotene, every day, and a special toothpaste formulated for dry mouth, PreviDent 5000 Dry Mouth, that I get from my dentist. I keep Biotene spray on my bedside table so I can use it during the night.

**Memory Loss**

Cancer patients and survivors call it *chemo brain* or *chemo fog*, meaning the cognitive and memory problems that can occur during and after cancer treatment. It's not clear what causes these memory changes. Symptoms differ among individuals, but mine included:

Difficulty concentrating—*What was I writing?*

Forgetting details of recent events —*Yes, we had a lovely dinner for my birthday at, at, at . . .!*

Feeling mentally slow—*Maybe I need more coffee?*

Forgetting or mixing up dates and appointments—*Your appointment is on Monday, not today.* Oops.

Losing my shit, in that I literally couldn't find my stuff—*Where did I put my book? It was right here.*

Losing words in mid . . . thought—*Where was I going with that?*

Speak to your doctor if you experience symptoms of memory loss or have difficulty concentrating.

To help get out of the fog, I kept a memo pad on my desk to keep track of tasks and I put appointments in my calendar as soon as I made them so I didn't forget or mix them up.

## Products

I have spoken to many cancer patients and survivors about what products should be used for the home, for skincare, for hair care, and for makeup following treatment. I have found no consensus on this topic.

Broadly, I have encountered three camps: the *all organic, all natural, no chemicals in my house or body ever again* camp, the *continue as we were* camp, and the hybrid camp, which combines elements of both. I fall in the hybrid camp, and since I've been asked many times, I've listed some of my favorite makeup and skincare products in *Resources*. Regardless of what camp you put yourself in, there's an app for that too!

For example, the Environmental Working Group's Healthy Living App allows users to scan a bar code for food and skincare products and review their ratings to help users make *healthier and more sustainable product choices*. Similarly, Think Dirty, Shop Clean is another app that helps consumer identify possible risks associated with their personal care products. The Dirty Dozen app does the same thing for produce (please see *Resources*).

## Scanxiety

Scanxiety is a term used to describe the anxiety, worry and fear that arise before and during cancer imaging scan and while waiting for results. Ask any survivor; these feelings can be intense and frightening. I could pop Xanax like M&M's while waiting for test results. I was comforted to learn that scanxiety wasn't in my head.

A study published in the *Journal of Clinical Oncology* confirmed:

*Although follow-up exams after completion of rigorous treatment including surgery or chemotherapy would be considered as an easy, uncomplicated part of the cancer treatment process, the anxiety surrounding having scans,* scanxiety, *often overwhelmed many cancer survivors resulting in poor quality of life.*

If you experience anxiety, stress, and fear when it's time for your tests, talk to your doctor about what can be done about it.

# Chapter 18
## Be Okay

To Do
Rethink applying for mother-of-the-year award
Find a shrink
Stop screaming

I HAVE MY NEXT three-month check-up with Dr. Abbasi in the morning. My nerves no longer fray at this thought. I accept that these appointments cause me anxiety every time they happen. I recognize when fear starts gnawing at me, making me snippy with Tim and the kids, I pause and apologize.

⤿

Sitting wrapped in a chair in our family room, I set down the Sunday *New York Times* to watch Tom tend the fire in the fireplace next to me. Tom places another log over the embers, squats down, then blows on the rising flames. The fire leaps to life—his mad Scout skills come in handy still.

Tom sits on the floor next to me and sprawls his upper body

across the chair's ottoman, his head next to my knee. He's exhausted from a weekend of swimming. I rub his back and breathe in the muskiness of him. We are content just to be, warm and at peace by the fire.

*We traveled a lifetime to get here.*

⌒

About a year after I'd finished treatment in March 2017, I took Tom, who had recently turned sixteen, for his annual physical. After I waited for a few minutes on the bench outside of the exam room, Tom's pediatrician joined me and offered me a form.

"This is a scale we use to see if our teens are exhibiting any signs of depression. As you can see from his answers, it seems that Tom is depressed. Have you noticed anything at home?" he asked.

"What? What do you mean 'Tom's depressed?'"

Cold panic filled my chest.

My eyes scanned the document. Tom had indicated on the form that he felt sad much of the time, hopeless, and had lost interest in the family and his activities. He didn't see the point of school. He wasn't interested in Scouts or swimming. He had trouble concentrating. After I finished reading the form the doctor gave me, I shook my head.

*Dear God, how did I miss this?*

"Not really. I mean, other than he seemed to want to sleep more than normal, but I thought he was worn out from school and swimming. He never said anything to me."

"Most of the time, kids don't. I think he needs to start counseling and probably should go on medication. Why don't we go in and talk to Tom?"

Back in the exam room, Tom slouched on the table, his head between his hands—his posture in sharp contrast to the smiling Disney characters that lined the walls.

I walked over to his side lifted his chin up, then asked, "Sweetie, why didn't you tell me you felt sad? How long have you felt this way?"

Tom paused for a moment and said, "Because you couldn't have handled it, Mom. Not with everything else that was going on. I've probably felt this way for over a year."

"A year, a whole year? Oh baby."

I wrapped my arms around him, and he started to cry.

As soon as I felt his tears against my skin, they set off a slew of memories—bits of conversation, dropped hints—from that year that passed through my brain. I understood his behavior now: why he often skipped practice, why he didn't go to Scouts, why he repeatedly complained about how *pointless* and *stupid* school seemed, why he had complained of stomach problems in the morning, and why he holed himself up in his room. He had exhibited some of the most common signs of depression in adolescents: loss of interest in activities, feeling hopeless and sleeping excessively. I didn't see his suffering because I'd been wrapped up in my own.

"I didn't want you to worry about me," he sobbed. "I figured I'd handle it, you know?"

"We're going to get you help," I said as I held him close, my child, not yet a man.

Of all the pain I'd experienced over the years, Tom's revelation pierced my heart the worst, a low tidemark in my life as a mom. I couldn't believe that he felt he had to protect me.

"We're going to get you better, Tom," his doctor said, then turned to me. "Do you have a therapist? He should also see a psychiatrist because he'll need medication."

"Yes, we have both. I'll call them when we get home."

⌒

From the time he was three, Tom had needed therapy to address developmental delays, processing disorders, executive function limitations, and ADHD. For the first year of high school, he seemed balanced and happy, even in the face of my breast cancer diagnosis.

Visits to his therapists had decreased by his freshman year to an *as needed* basis.

Had I focused more on Tom's withdrawal from the family and his activities and pressed him about how he felt at the time, perhaps we could have gotten him help sooner and set him on a path to healing. As it was, it took a year of therapy and medication to get Tom back to the outgoing, funny, and engaged teen he had been.

I can't ever give him back that lost year. I can't ever erase the memory of the pain I feel I caused him.

In my tunnel vision and determination to get back to *normal life*, I failed to see the impact my illness had on my family, and on Tom in particular. I didn't connect the dots. Now, I saw his moodiness and isolation from the family were huge signs—red flags—and I walked right past them. I chalked it up to him being *a typical teenager*. Had Tom's moodiness, need to sleep, or withdrawal occurred only sporadically, perhaps my perception of the situation may not have been wrong. But it was way more than that.

I'm not a doctor or psychologist or therapist. I have no formal training in child development (for the record, I'm not giving professional advice). I can only speak to my experiences, and based on them, I can't emphasize this enough: *Keep an eye on the kids as you go through your experience. Don't assume they're all right because they don't want to talk about how they're feeling, particularly teens.*

Talk with partners or spouses about their own observations of them, because theirs likely will be clearer than the potential patient's. Check in with teachers, coaches, parents of your children's close friends, or other trusted adults who come into regular contact with them to see if they've noticed any *off* behaviors and enlist their support to be another set of eyes. If you think there's an issue, don't wait to seek professional help.

By the end of the year, my post-treatment anxiety was spiraling out of control, particularly as I got closer to my check-ups with Dr. Abbasi. One evening in December, Tim noticed my mood tank as I harped on the boys.

"James. Thomas. For the love of God, take the wet boots off at the door. It's not hard. The mat is at the door for a reason. You're wrecking the floors that were just cleaned. Now I have to wipe them down again. Come on!!"

James cringed as I continued to raise my voice.

"Why do I have to remind you to do this over and over again?"

"Sorry, Mom," he whispered as he took off his boots and fled from the kitchen.

*Why do I keep doing this? They're just being kids. I have to calm down.*

Tim sat me down on the leather sofa in the family room and looked me in the eye.

"When's your next appointment with Dr. Abbasi?"

"In a couple of days. Why?"

"It shows."

"What do you mean?"

"I mean you're losing your shit again. This has to stop, Chris. We can't live like this, wondering when you're going to lose it."

I looked away and rubbed my palm across my forehead. Tim took my hand.

"You can't keep blowing up over little things. The boys can't stand it when you yell. I can't stand it either. Please, sweetie."

I pulled Tim's arm around me, curled up against him, and sighed.

"I know. I'm sorry. I don't know what's wrong with me. These appointments make me anxious. I think...I think I need to find a therapist."

"You do whatever you need to get back to you. We want you back—loving, kind you. Not bat-shit-screaming you."

"Tim, I know. I hate this. I can't live like this anymore. I can't freak out every time I have to see Dr. Abbasi. I'll ask him if he can refer me to someone."

A few days later, I spoke to Dr. Abbasi.

"I can't stand it. I'm stressed every time I have to see you and wait for my blood test results. I'm scared about the results. I feel like I need to take Xanax every single day, and I'm taking it out on everyone in my house. This has to stop. I need to start seeing a therapist. Can you recommend anyone?"

He wrote down a name and handed me the paper.

"He's very good and a friend. Tell him I recommended him to you. Chris, what you're feeling is common. I think you're having a harder time than most because of all you went through as a teen. Text me and let me know when you have your first appointment."

"I will. Thanks."

As soon as I got home I called the doctor's office. He wasn't taking new patients at the time, even with referrals from Dr. Abbasi.

*There has to be someone in the area who deals with cancer. I live near a major medical center, for Pete's sake. I want to see a psychiatrist with experience with cancer patients.*

Putting my research skills to the test, I turned to Google with a search, *psychiatrist cancer patients NJ*, and within a nanosecond found Dr. Roger Granet—a psychiatrist who only took care of cancer patients and who also was, wait for it, a published author of not only books about dealing with cancer, but also, wait for it, poetry. I didn't know about the poetry part right away, but I couldn't have found a more perfect psychiatrist for me if I had dropped on my knees and prayed for a miracle. Happily, he was taking new patients.

And so it began, my path to living a less anxious life. When I walked in Dr. Granet's office, I didn't know what to expect. I found a tall, handsome, and tanned doctor in the standard dress slacks, button-down shirt, tie, and loafers that all my docs tend to sport. Dr. Granet had warm brown eyes behind his glasses and a smile that reminded me of a cup of tea—one that would simply let me talk.

And dear God, did I talk.

⌒

Starting with every week, then moving to every two weeks then three weeks, then months in time, I met with Dr. Granet and, not without trepidation, opened the Box of Hodgkin's memories that I'd taped closed years ago. One by one, I brought them out into the light of day. I learned those unexamined, unprocessed, and solidly repressed memories intensified my present-day angst. I also learned—sadly—that I would never eliminate feeling stressed when I went for a follow-up appointment, although I would learn to manage my feelings of apprehension.

I unpacked each memory from my teenage Hodgkin's experience and, in time, wrote about many of them. On some days, those memories overwhelmed me.

⌒

One spring day as I wrote about my treatment for Hodgkin's, the smell of the hospital from long ago suddenly filled my mind and nose. That scent had made me sick when I was a patient, and years later when I returned for my follow-up visits. I hadn't thought about that smell since 1984, when I walked out of Memorial Sloan Kettering for the last time.

I broke into a cold sweat, placed my head on my desk, and clutched my stomach as wave after wave of nausea passed through me. I leaned over the kitchen sink and dry-heaved.

When the nausea ended, I called Dr. Granet and explained what happened.

"Why are these memories so hard? I was literally sick over this sickly-sweet smell I remembered from when I was a kid."

"Chris, smell is one of the most powerful forms of memory. You felt sick because you remembered being sick when you were exposed to that scent, which was a commonly used disinfectant at the time."

"But I haven't thought about that smell in over thirty years. Wait, I remember something now. That smell was the reason why I hated going back to Memorial Sloan Kettering for my checkups. The awful odor hit me as soon as I opened the doors and made me sick every time I went. I'm still feeling sick talking to you about it. Why is this so hard?"

"Why do you think it's hard?"

"You know, I hate when you do that." I paused, listening to my doctor's silence.

Dr. Granet wasn't going to answer my question, I'd learned that much over several months of therapy. I had to answer it myself. I sighed.

"It's hard because I didn't deal with it then. I did what I was supposed to do, what my parents expected me to do: be a brave little soldier. I went to treatment and I didn't complain. My parents had to have known how awful it was for me, but I just had to get through it. And it hurts, Dr. Granet. It hurts so much."

I couldn't stop the tears from falling.

"And now you're feeling it, Chris. Fear, anger with your parents, the memory of that awful smell—they're feelings, that's all. And, yes, they hurt, but now that you've felt them, you're free of them."

"You think? I don't feel free right now. I feel awful."

"What you're doing is hard work. It takes a lot of courage. And it's harder for you because now you're writing about the experiences. Know that you're going to live a healthier, happier life because each time you feel, really feel, one of these memories, it loses its power over you. You're a resilient woman."

"Thank you for saying so. I think I'm okay now. But I can't write anymore today."

I ended the call, washed my face, threw on a sweater and decided to get a manicure. The next day, I sat at my desk, opened my document on my computer, and paused, my fingers hovering over the keyboard.

Dr. Granet was right. When I just started describing the smells of the hospital again, I didn't get sick or nauseous.

More than anything else, psychotherapy has given me safe place to face my demons, look them squarely in the eye, and send them on their way. It's given me a better understanding of how I dealt with having cancer and how to live my best life. I wish I'd gotten help sooner and spared my family my screaming.

⤳

We all come up with ways to get through and to cope with cancer. Cancer—as awful as it is—doesn't require us to be miserable or to make others miserable. That's not to say we have to feel happy all the time or sprinkle rainbow glitter dust over our days. But there is something to be said about living with equanimity. Joan Halifax, the Buddhist Roshi, explained that *equanimity* is *grounded in the experience of letting go.* Equanimity gives us the capacity *to be in touch with suffering and at the same time not be swept away by it* and allows us to live with loving-kindness and to radiate calm, peace, and trust. No wonder it's one of Dr. Granet's favorite words.

And it's become one of mine, too.

⤳

Living with equanimity has taught me to let go—to let go of the people, things, and obligations that are no longer meaningful, and to accept those things I cannot change about my post-cancer life.

⤳

## The Practical Reality
### Loss of Friendship

Losing a long-term friendship after my diagnosis was one of the saddest and most painful things that happened to me. More than anything else, survivors have told me they wished they knew this loss might happen as a result of their diagnosis. Based on the many conversations I've had, it happens more often than I would have thought.

When speaking about loss of friendships, I've heard some survivors say, *It wasn't about me. It's them.* True enough. I've heard others say, *You find out who your real friends are.* Also, true enough. But, I've found that there's more to the loss of friendships than either of those statements reveal.

To begin, yes, it *is* about them. I was told that friends withdraw from relationships after learning that their friend or loved one has cancer because they're afraid. Cancer forces anyone who comes into contact with it to confront their own mortality, fears, and perhaps memories of the deaths—whether cancer-related or not—of other loved ones. For some people, it's too much to handle.

While cancer taught me who my real friends were, it also taught me who they weren't. I've learned who and what's important in my life. After I got over my sadness and anger at the loss of someone I thought was a true friend, I let the relationship go.

# Chapter 19
## Arrived

IT'S MARCH 3ᴿᴰ—TOM'S eighteenth birthday—and a little over three years to the day I heard the words I hadn't ever wanted to hear again. And like the day Tom was born, we're waiting for a big winter storm—the season's final send-off before spring muscles her way in with warming days and puddles to muddy the flowerbeds and return my little corner of the world to life. I gaze at the slushy ice on the patio, wishing this storm would pass us by, as it did on the day Tom entered the world, and as I prayed when I received the phone call I feared.

I'm desperate for the promise of sun and its warmth.

Breathing in the cinnamon and clove-scented applesauce I'm cooking for Tom's birthday dinner, I check the online weather report. Leaving my computer to pay attention to the pot of bubbling applesauce, I dip in a spoon and taste—a bit too sweet. Grabbing a lemon from the fridge, I slice it, squeeze the juice into the pan, then stir. Tasting it again, I think, *better*, because a little sour cuts the sweet.

And perhaps, that's what I was meant to learn from my second dance with the Beast: to accept the sweet and the sour, each in its own right and time, and to recognize that I had no control over it anyway, years of list-making notwithstanding. I had to return to my past—to the scared and lonely teenager with her notebook and Stevie Nicks albums. I had to face the fears that dwelt within me and forgive my parents for their secret-keeping (that I understand all too well now) to get to this place of mostly peace.

While this is not the life I would have planned, organized, or listed for my family or me, this life is ours, even though it comes with scars, radiation tattoos, medication, and lingering fear of recurrence and metastases. My life comes with aortic valve stenosis from calcifications to my heart caused by my teenage radiation therapy, which will require heart surgery sooner than I'd hoped. But, I try, at the urging of my Catholic, turned Buddhist, law school dear one, *to seek peaceful coexistence with the undesired.*

I will face all of it, I hope, with grace, courage, and good humor, not because I want to, but because I must. Does this mean I stopped all my yelling? I wish. But I do try to catch myself and consider the alternative. Sometimes it works, sometimes, not. The point is that I try to pause—whether it's over something my kids did or didn't do or over *that* driver on I-287—and consider how or even whether to respond. I'm learning to let my life move in its own season, to tend it with a gentle hand as a loving gardener does, and to be kinder to others and myself, for we are only stewards on this glorious, imperfect planet. Or as my dad often joked with his hearty gallows laughter, *None of us gets out of this life alive.*

The snow has arrived, swirling flakes outside the windows, again blanketing my garden beds in frozen silence. Yet, I know that beneath the snow and the ice, bulbs are starting to stir and blades of grass are beginning to unfurl, waiting for the moment to push through to the light, again.

# Sources

Breastcancer.org. (2015, March 5). *Before You Begin Chemotherapy*. Retrieved from https://www.breastcancer.org/treatment/chemotherapy/process/before.

Breastcancer.org. (2019, March 9). *Hand-Foot Syndrome (HFS) or Palmar-Plantar Erythrodysesthesia (PPE)*. Retrieved from https://www.breastcancer.org/treatment/side_effects/hand_foot_synd

Breastcancer.org. (2019, March 9). *Lymphedema*. Retrieved from https://www.breastcancer.org/treatment/lymphedema

Breastcancer.org. (2019, March 9). *Neuropathy*. Retrieved from https://www.breastcancer.org/treatment/side_effects/neuropathy

Cancer.Net (2018, May). *Dehydration*. Retrieved from https://www.cancer.net/navigating-cancer-care/side-effects/dehydration

Cho, Juhee *et al.* "Scanxiety and Quality of Life among Breast Cancer Survivors." *Journal of Clinical Oncology*, vol. 33, no. 15, 31 Jan. 2017, suppl, http://ascopubs.org/doi/abs/10.1200/jco.2015.33.15_suppl.e20569

Granet, Roger, M.D. *Surviving Cancer Emotionally: Learning How to Heal*. New York: John Wiley & Sons, 2001.

Hanai, Akiko *et al.* "Effects of Cryotherapy on Objective and Subjective Symptoms of Paclitaxel-Induced Neuropathy: Prospective Self-Controlled Trial." *Journal of the National Cancer Institute*, vol. 110, no. 2, 1 Feb. 2018, pp. 141–148, https://doi.org/10.1093/jnci/djx178

Halifax, Joan. (2012, December 20). "Equanimity: The Fourth Abode." Upaya Zen Center. Retrieved from https://www.upaya.org/2012/12/equanimity-the-fourth-abode-joan-halifax-roshi/

Johns Hopkins Medicine. *Keep Your Brain Young with Music.* Retrieved from https://www.hopkinsmedicine.org/health/ healthy_aging/healthy_mind/keep-your-brain-young-with-music

Lymphatic Education and Research Network. *FAQs about the Lymphatic System.* Retrieved from https://lymphaticnetwork. org/living-with-lymphedema/lymphatic-disease/

Lymphatic Education and Research Network. *FAQs about the Lymphadema.* Retrieved from https://lymphaticnetwork.org/ living-with-lymphedema/lymphedema/

Mayo Clinic. *Edema.* Retrieved from https://www.mayoclinic.org/ diseases-conditions/edema/symptoms-causes/syc-20366493

Meyer, Dan and Diane. *To Know by Experience.* Morganton: Artcraft Press, 1972.

# Resources

Some resources I used are listed below. This list is, by no means, all-inclusive. For more resources, visit my website: https://christineshieldscorrigan.com/.

## Books I Love

Brosch, Allie. *Hyperbole and a Half: Unfortunate Situations, Flawed Coping Mechanisms, Mayhem, and Other Things That Happened.* New York: Simon & Schuster, 2013.

A laugh out loud, beautifully illustrated, collection of essays about life. And dogs. Includes an exquisite piece about living with depression.

Goldberg, Natalie. *Writing Down to the Bones: Freeing the Writer Within.* Boulder: Shambala, 2016.

Craft book with suggestions, encouragement, and advice on writing from *first thoughts*, on using verbs, on overcoming doubts, and even on choosing a restaurant in which to write.

Granet, Roger, M.D. *Surviving Cancer Emotionally: Learning How to Heal.* New York: John Wiley & Sons, 2001.

Advice book written with compassion and clarity by a psychiatrist specializing in the care and treatment of cancer patients. Addresses coping with every stage of the disease and how to turn a devastating illness into a catalyst for positive change.

Guntupalli, Saketh, M.D. & Karinch, Maryanne. *Sex and Cancer: Intimacy, Romance, and Love after Diagnosis and Treatment.* Lanham: Rowman & Littlefield Publishers (2017).

Advice book that focuses on overcoming the challenges of sexual dysfunction after a cancer diagnosis.

Lamott, Anne. *Bird by Bird: Some Instructions on Writing and Life.* New York: Pantheon Books, 1994.

My go to craft book that has had a place on my desk for twenty-five years—even when I was a practicing lawyer—with insightful, funny, and poignant moments and excellent writing advice.

Lamott, Anne. *Help Thanks Wow: The Three Essential Prayers.* New York: Riverhead Books, 2012.

Prayer simplified.

Servan-Schreiber, David, M.D. *Anticancer: A New Way of Life.* New York: Viking, 2009.

Addresses how to develop a science-based anticancer diet; how to reap the benefits of exercise, yoga, and meditation; which toxic, unsafe products to replace in your home; and how to stave off the effects of helplessness and unhealed wounds to regain balance.

Wiederkehr, *Seven Sacred Pauses: Living Mindfully Through the Hours of the Day.* Notre Dame: Sorin Books, 2008.

Devotional that uses scripture, poetry, reflections, personal stories, and quotes from spiritual teachers for many religions to help readers learn to live in the present moment and appreciate the rich tradition of the sacred hours.

# Bras for Reconstructed Breasts

### AnaOno LLC
anaono.com

Lingerie, swimwear, and loungewear made for women with breast cancer by women with breast cancer. Includes solutions for women with breast reconstruction, breast surgery, mastectomy, or who are living with other conditions that cause pain or discomfort.

## Cancer Organizations

### American Cancer Society
cancer.org

Nationwide, community-based, voluntary health organization dedicated to eliminating cancer as a major health problem through research, education, and advocacy. Provides a variety of programs and support to cancer patients, their caregivers, and families.

### Breastcancer.org
breastcancer.org

Nonprofit dedicated to providing the most reliable, complete, and up-to-date information about breast cancer. Its mission is to help women, men, and their loved ones make sense of the complex medical and personal information about breast health and breast cancer, so they can make the best decisions for their lives.

**American Institute for Cancer Research**

aicr.org

Focuses on the link between diet and cancer. Funds research in the field of nutrition, physical activity and cancer prevention, treatment and survival and educates the public about its research.

**Diva for a Day**

divaforaday.org

Nonprofit that provides a day of beauty and pampering to women dealing with cancer.

**Leukemia & Lymphoma Society**

lls.org

Nonprofit dedicated to curing leukemia, lymphoma, Hodgkin's disease, and myeloma, and improving the quality of life of patients and their families. Funds blood cancer research around the world and provides free information and support services.

**Living Beyond Breast Cancer**

lbbc.org

Nonprofit that works with women who have been diagnosed with breast cancer and their caregivers throughout their experience of diagnosis, treatment, and recovery.

**National Cancer Institute**

cancer.gov

Is the federal government's principal agency for cancer research and training and part of the National Institutes of Health. Provides comprehensive information regarding cancer causes, prevention, treatment, and care for individuals with cancer.

## Mastectomy/Nipple Tattoo Artists

**Beth Fairchild**
bethfairchild@icloud.com

**Sarah Peacock**
Artfuel Tattoo Shop & Art Gallery
2165 Wrightsville Avenue
Wilmington, NC 28403
910-343-5233

**Pink Ink Tattoo LLC**
pinkinktattoo.com

## Products I Love

### Brow/Lash Serum/Makeup

Coola Mineral Liplux Organic Tinted Lip Balm, SPF 30
Available at: coola.com

Nulastin Brow
Available at: nulastin.com

Rodan & Fields Enhancements Lash Boost
Available at: rodanandfields.com

Thrive Causemetics
Available at: thrivecausemetics.com

**Moisturizers**

Anti-Aging Body Balm
Undaria Algae Oil
Available at: oseamalibu.com

Burt's Bees Ultra Conditioning Lip Balm
Available at: Most retailers

Udderly Smooth Hand Cream
Available at: Most retailers

**Personal Lubricant**

Astroglide Gel Personal Lubricant
Available at: Most retailers

KY Warming Liquid Personal Lubricant
Available at: Most retailers

## Sunscreen

Coola Suncare Sport Classic Sunscreen, Unscented, SPF 50
Coola Suncare Body Sunscreen Spray, Guava Mango, SPF 30
Available at: coola.com

## Professional Organizations

**Academy of Nutrition and Dietetics**
eatright.org

Provides referrals to registered dieticians and information about nutrition.

**American Psychiatric Association**

psychiatry.org

Provides information about common mental disorders, including symptoms, risk factors and treatment options, as well as referrals to psychiatrists.

**American Psychological Association**

apa.org

Provides information related to psychological issues affecting individuals' daily physical and emotional well-being, as well as referrals to psychologists.

**Cancer.Net - American Society of Clinical Oncology**

cancer.net

Provides timely, comprehensive information to help patients and families make informed health care decisions, as well as referrals to oncologists.

## There's An App for That

The following apps are available for download from itunes.apple.com or play.google.com.

**Calm Meditation and Sleep Stories**

An app for meditation, relaxation and sleep.

**Environmental Working Group's Health Living**

Gives product health and safety ratings for 200,000 food and cosmetic products

**Insight Timer**

An app to help with sleep, anxiety, and stress

# Acknowledgments

ILLNESS AND WRITING ARE often solitary, but the acts of recovering and sharing one's writing require others. I have been graced with an abundance of family, friends, outstanding medical professionals, and mentors without whom I would not have seen this day.

Thank you to the army of friends and family who prayed for us, made meals for us, sent flowers, wrote letters and cards, drove my kids to school and to practice, flocked our lawn, visited me, planted flowers, read drafts, and more: Cathi and Samantha Askin, Back to Nature Nursery (especially Shannon Crossman and Amy Seuberth), Elizabeth and Mark Barickman, Margaret Barrett, Billy Beyer, Wendy Boudreau, Stephanie Caesar, Nancy Clerici, Bob and Julie Corrigan, Kevin and Lina Corrigan, Jeanne Corrigan, Paul Corrigan, Reverend Monsignor Sylvester Cronin, Maureen Dazzo, Elaine Edge, Debra Esposito, Kara Falivene, Jackie Gattoni, Peggy Glennon, Peg Harmon, Rich Heller, Bruce and Teresa Henshall, Father Walter Jenkins, Jane Ikeda, Diane Kiel, Jane Kolarik, Kathy Krell, Maureen Johnson,

Laura Laurita, Athena Lee, Kris Leopold, Stacy Lettie, Kimberly Lopez, Danielle Lumby, Cindy Malatesta, Allison McCabe, Alyson McCauley, Susie McGeough, Laura McInerney, Diana Mentone, Barbara Miller, Kathy Morgan, Sue Morrissey, Trina Moumblow, Kay Mullins, John and Linda Musacchio, Richard Poccia, Melissa Pruskowski, Barbara Ring, Carla Risoldi, Susan Roos, St. James Church, Somerset Hills YMCA Swim Team, Coaches, and Swim Team Parents Organization, Katie Straub, Tom and Maria Sullivan, Tim's Partners, Joanne Wachenfeld, Shannon Waters, Ria and Mike Zazzarino, and Christine Ziegler.

Thank you to the best damn team of doctors and nurses I could have hoped for as a teen: Dr. Frank Forte and the medical professionals at Staten Island University Hospital and Memorial Sloan Kettering Cancer Center; and as an adult: my oncologist, Muhammad R. Abbasi, M.D. of Oncology and Hematology Specialists, my breast surgeon, William Diehl, M.D., and nurse navigator, Karen Loewen, R.N., of Summit Medical Group, my psychiatrist, Roger Granet, M.D., my plastic surgeon, Farhad Rafizadeh, M.D. of Better Plastic Surgery, and the outstanding nursing staff and health care professionals at Morristown Medical Center.

Thank you to the precious infusion friends I made along the way: Karen Boyle, Karen Gordon, and Laura Marschall.

Thank you to the many strong, spirited, and compassionate survivors who have been generous with their time, stories, and support: Chiara D'Agostino (may her memory be a blessing), Dana Donofree, Beth Fairchild, Nora McMahon, Rachel Park, and Tara Williamson.

Thank you to the outstanding publishing team at Koehler Books, especially John Koehler and Joe Coccaro for believing in this book and taking a chance on a new author, and Becky Hilliker for her sharp editorial insights and patience.

I treasure the advice, guidance, and insight of the instructors and coaches who have taught me much over these years: Melissa Petro,

Kerry Cohen, Randon Billings Noble, Lisa Romeo, Cullen Thomas, and, most especially, Ryder S. Ziebarth, without whom I would have never finished this book. I'm grateful to the editors who gave me the chance to write and have supported my work, especially: Erin Khar, Kat McNichol, Nathan Primeau, Amy Roost, Joanell Serra, April Stearns, and Allison K Williams. A thousand thanks to Elizabeth Zack for her keen editing and to Lilly Dancyger for her structural insights as I struggled through early drafts. I appreciate the many wonderful writers who have shared their time, words, and wisdom: Jacqui Boulter, Marcia Bilyk, Olga Christie, Laraine Herring, Min Jin Lee, and Kitta MacPherson.

Thank you to Sister M. William McGovern, who first taught me the power of writing.

Thank you to my parents. I wish I could hand this book to you. I pray it would make you proud. I miss you both every day.

I am grateful for my sister, Jennifer, whose care for me mirrored our mother's, and to my brother, Marty, who still makes me laugh.

I have no words to thank my husband, Tim, for his infinite patience, abiding love, and well-timed punch line. To my children, Kate, Tom, and James, I know there were many days when you wished I'd chosen another path, but I'm forever grateful that you walked with me along this one, a testament to your courage and resilience. I love you always.

And, if I've forgotten anyone here, my heart and soul have not; please forgive me.

# About the Author

A GRADUATE OF FORDHAM University School of Law and Manhattan College, Christine Shields Corrigan built a successful two-decade career as a labor and employment law attorney, then as a legal writer and editor. After surviving cancer in midlife, Chris became a freelance writer and cancer patient advocate.

Chris's nonfiction work has appeared in various anthologies, including *The Writer's Circle 2, The Potato Soup Journal Anthology, and (Her)oics: Women's Lived Experiences During the Coronavirus Pandemic,* and in popular and literary media, including *Ravishly. com, Grown & Flown, Purple Clover, Wildfire Magazine, Brevity Blog,* and elsewhere.

She lives in Somerset County, New Jersey with her family and devoted Cavalier King Charles spaniel. Chris serves on the programming committee of the Morristown Festival of Books, teaches creative nonfiction writing for a local adult education program, and provides writing workshops for cancer support groups. When she's not writing, Chris works in her garden and enjoys reading and cooking.